I0127356

AFRICAN SON

William J. Hemminger

University Press of America,® Inc.
Lanham · Boulder · New York · Toronto · Plymouth, UK

Copyright © 2012 by
University Press of America,® Inc.
4501 Forbes Boulevard
Suite 200
Lanham, Maryland 20706
UPA Acquisitions Department (301) 459-3366

10 Thornbury Road
Plymouth PL6 7PP
United Kingdom

All rights reserved
Printed in the United States of America
British Library Cataloging in Publication Information Available

Library of Congress Control Number: 2012931663
ISBN: 978-0-7618-5843-0 (paperback : alk. paper)
eISBN: 978-0-7618-5844-7

♾™ The paper used in this publication meets the minimum
requirements of American National Standard for Information
Sciences—Permanence of Paper for Printed Library Materials,
ANSI Z39.48-1992

To Jill, Johanna, and Mollie, who have shared so many of these experiences with me.

To my African family of friends, all of whom have taught me so much.

And to the Fulbright Association, which made many of these experiences possible.

CONTENTS

PREFACE

These personal essays reflect my many years' experience in Africa. In the mid-1970s I served as a Peace Corps volunteer in Senegal where I taught English and mathematics and organized a public library in the town of Dagana along the Senegal River. I spent the summer after my first year of teaching in Saneinte, a small village in the interior, where I taught French to villagers. Years later my wife Jill and daughter Johanna went with me to live in the capital city of Madagascar, Antananarivo, where as a Fulbright scholar I taught courses in American language and literature at the national university during two academic years. With a group of US academics I spent the summer of 1993 traveling and studying in South Africa, Zimbabwe, and Malawi. Most recently, a Fulbright grant permitted me and my family—now including two daughters, Johanna and Mollie—to live in Yaoundé, Cameroon, where I worked at University of Yaoundé I during the 2004-5 academic year. These longer stays have been complemented by shorter trips to Cameroon and Senegal. The map on page x identifies African nations to which the essays make reference; other, more detailed maps appear when pertinent throughout the text.

All place names and locations are as exact as I have been able to record or recollect. I have, however, changed the names of some people in the interests of privacy. Events have been recounted as faithfully and accurately as I could, though I have rearranged a few details for the purposes of art or argument. I have tried to be consistent in the spelling of place-names and foreign words, a rather hopeless endeavor. Most such names I learned in their francophone forms, so, for example, the Bénoué River is also known on maps as Benue (and is an important river and region in Nigeria under that spelling of its name). Words from Wolof or other languages I have transcribed into the phonology of contemporary American English to the best of my abilities. My apologies to native speakers and to rigorous linguists.

It is my hope that these essays convey to the reader at least a glimpse of the great panorama of life in Africa.

ACKNOWLEDGMENTS

I owe a huge debt of gratitude to Dave Schlea for helping with the production of this book in so many ways—as graphic designer, cover designer, and publishing consultant.

Thanks to many African friends—among them Richard, Christy, Maalik—who welcomed me into their homes and lives and helped make many of the experiences chronicled in this book possible.

Thanks also to my wife Jill for her love and support—not to mention her careful reading, copious notes, and copy editing.

"Grass" was previously published in *Interdisciplinary Studies in Literature and Environment* 11.2 (Summer 2004), pages 186-89.

And, finally, thanks to the University Press of America for letting *African Son* see the light of day.

ALGERIA

MAURITANIA

MALI

SENEGAL

SIERRA LEONE

CAMEROON

GULF OF
GUINEA

TANZANIA

MALAWI

MOZAMBIQUE

ZAMBIA

ZIMBABWE

MADAGASCAR

SOUTH
ATLANTIC
OCEAN

SOUTH
AFRICA

INDIAN
OCEAN

0   400   800   1200 km

0   200 400 600 800 mi

Chapter One
A Friend of the Family

The death of a child is the worst, and I felt somehow responsible. I had told his parents, in my halting but passable Wolof, "Give him half of a tablet today, the other half tomorrow." I feared that they might overdose the boy, shivering on the mat, his fever spiking. I wasn't even sure that it was malaria, but all the standard symptoms were there.

"He needs lots of water," I told them. That instruction sent his sisters to the river to collect water in their broad pans enameled in wild swirls of color. Not exactly clean water: people come daily to bathe and do their laundry, and lean zebu lumber down to drink and relieve themselves. The water was collected, carried home, and poured into large jugs called *canaris* that sit in the corners of all the inhabited huts. I doubted the wisdom of my instruction: if the malaria didn't get him, dysentery or schistosomiasis might.

His family depended on me, and for a 21-year-old, that dependence is gratifying. My first family.

There was his father, Abdou Diop. He was lucky enough to have a paying job. Each morning Abdou and a small group of men from the village gathered on the macadam road outside of town awaiting the truck from the sugar plantation to come by and pick them up. The men were carted to a village about 30 clicks up the road—and up the river—where a French firm had irrigated many hundreds of hectares and started a very profitable sugar plantation in the desert. Jobs for hundreds of villagers and the possibility of money: a chance to eat more than dried fish and beans over grainy millet, maybe the possibility of paying school fees for one of the kids.

But God, it was awful work. Slashing the stiff sugar cane, leaving behind row after row of dangerously sharp stalks that sliced easily through calloused feet. Sloshing through the oozy sand, home to snakes, under the unyielding sun, never shielded with a cloud. Yet it was work.

I got to see the other side of the operation. The only non-African resident in the whole region, I was invited to meet the French boss, Dupont, and his American wife.

The Duponts lived for a few months of the year in a compound that housed themselves and the other *toubab* managers of the plant. The entire ensemble of homes was surrounded by a continuous cinder-block wall topped by shards of glass that sparkled eerily in the sun. The individual houses, electrified by a portable generator, were miniature tropical replicas of homes in France and England—filled with imported niceties, surrounded by pretty gardens that had to be watered twice daily.

I'll never forget the meal that I had there that day: turkey flown in from France, a Bordeaux wine, apples and chocolates—fantastical food. The dog, an insipid squalling poodle, was given a plate of turkey meat that could have fed a Senegalese family for a week or more. And the servant, gloved and taciturn (so unusual for the Wolofs), was a villager whom I knew from his own world: I had taught his kids, eaten at his family compound. I tried to joke a little with Abdoulaye before dinner, but the deference reserved for toubabs was turned on for me as well.

I have often wondered what Abdoulaye thought of me that day: Had I become one of the others—the rich and separate toubabs? Were my friendly relations with the villagers instantly proven spurious as I guzzled imported wine and ate fatted meat kept separate from hungry others outside the walled-and-protected compound? Or was this part of inscrutable toubab behavior, the ability to deal readily with contradictory experiences?

Abdoulaye wouldn't have guessed how uncomfortable I was at the Dupont party. What if the glass-capped walls had suddenly collapsed, letting the desert encroach upon these false oases of imported green? What if Abdou Diop's family knew what food was tossed the sniveling dog? What if there weren't such vast gaps between rich and poor, both represented in this strange world? These "what if" constructions became the unspoken grammar of the afternoon, regulating my involvement and hampering my enjoyment. But I was a good guest, praising the food and its preparation, toasting the hosts' generosity. "Come back—we can talk about America next time," Madame Dupont added in her New England accent. I thanked the Duponts but knew that I would not visit them again. It was funny to think how different my response to them would have been if the context of our meeting had been France or New England, not Senegal.

The word got out that I had been to see the toubabs, and oddly enough it seemed to increase my credibility among the villagers. To them it was clear that I was rich, despite my unfortunate wardrobe and relative material improvidence. After all, I was a toubab too. To be sure, on my 100-dollar-a-month Peace Corps salary, I was rich in a village where food was limited in quantity and kind and the variety of buyable material goods restricted pretty much to enameled pans and mosquito nets.

I learned quickly how to deal with this perception of me as a local relief organization. I found a couple of families and limited my largesse to them and their requests. One of these families was the family of Abdou Diop.

Abdou Diop used to come to my house just before the end of each month. Ritual greetings first—*Are you a peace? Is your family at peace?*—plus the repetition of my given last name: *Touré, Touré.* We'd spend ten or fifteen minutes exchanging these words, pressing our hands together, avoiding one another's eyes.

Then a shift in the incipient conversation. "The price of rice has gone up again. And the grains are broken at that," he'd say. Then Abdou Diop might note how the cooking oil had been depleted or how Baïdy's trip to the dispensary had cost more than expected. I learned that I needed to let him pronounce his problems but that, of course, he would never ask for help outright. And I also learned (or thought I learned) not to reach into my wallet directly and, by so doing, incarnate his claim on my relative economic security. I would tell him that I understood how difficult things were, excuse myself, call his eldest son over to my place a little while later, and ask Iba to deliver money to his father on my behalf. We went through this ritual practically every month. But it never made sense that Abdou's physical laboring each hot day brought him barely enough to keep his family in food and shelter while my salary—trivial by States' standards—more than generously supported me as I did work that I loved.

I felt that I was closest to his wife Maïmouna. She had told me that she was about 28 years old and had given birth eight times. I don't even remember how I found this information out, since most Wolofs make no mention of personal statistics. I guess I must one time have embarked on a crass questioning campaign, unearthing, in the western way, what is private, possibly secret, maybe better left unknown. Anyway, she talked easily to me despite the differences that separated us. Did it matter to her that I had spent four years in New York City at college? What was New York—or higher education—to her? Could she have understood that my mother was an alcoholic, that growing up for me offered much less of the family togetherness than, despite their poverty, her family enjoyed? Could she have known that I was afraid of assuming responsibility for another person, having grown up in a culture that encourages independence but neither care nor compassion?

Most times I could find her sitting on her mat spread on the dry dirt underneath the acacia tree, swatting flies away from one of the several infants in her care. She might chide me for not having stopped in the day before to greet the family properly (which always meant shaking each person's hand, sitting down under the thorny acacia tree, and talking for a while). Or she'd start in on the weather, interminably hot. And she was especially interested in my mother. *How does she live? Where does she live? Is she cared for properly?* Always the same questions concerning my mother. *Greet her for us. Tell her that we think of her.* Somewhere in northern Senegal today lives a young woman (born after I left the village) whose name is Hettie Maïmouna, a legacy to the lives of two remarkably different women.

Physically, Maïmouna's world was a small one—from the open door of the mud-brick hut to the acacia tree and from the acacia tree to the fire-ring. An ambit of about 20 feet in any direction at most. Occasionally she would get out of the compound and head to the river for water or washing or to the market, but usually she depended on one of the neighbor girls for those tasks. Maïmouna had her hands full looking after her five kids. Constant work, without any expectation of material improvement or the hope for any sort of break. All day long, at least one of the children sat strapped to her back as the woman poked the smoldering fire underneath the blackened cooking kettle, winnowed and picked over grains of rice in the thin shade of the acacia tree, or swept the sandy yard.

The youngest living child, Baïdy, spent much of his time sitting naked in the dirt and moaning. A weak, will-less moan. His belly was distended despite the powdered milk that I sent for and prepared especially for him. I half expected to wake up one day and find the family sitting in mourning, neighbors gathered uncannily by the silent noise of death in the village. Yet Baïdy hung on—month after month. What a testimony to the will-to-live, a force that refuses death despite dour circumstances of actual, lived life.

Baïdy would have made a suitable candidate for the photos that came out of Sahelian Africa at that time—bloated children sitting in squalor, with maybe a skeletal zebu and leafless thorn tree nearby. Everyone at home saw those pictures, and well-meaning folks sent many dollars to relief agencies. Many of those dollars came to line the pockets of local government officials; bags of US corn were sold to villagers despite the words emblazoned on the burlap—"gift of the US government." The mayor of our region got relatively rich on those gifts, this "redistribution of wealth." But Baïdy got no benefit from the international relief effort.

So I began to reserve a portion of my end-of-the-month check for the Diop family. I cannot say whether my motive was an atavistic *noblesse oblige*. But when mangoes came in season, I bought kilos and sent them next door. When dates came on camel-back from desert oases in Mauritania, I sent over heavy, sticky bunches. Rice, powdered milk, cooking oil too. For the first time in my life I became a provider.

The giving had two important and unexpected effects. Maïmouna insisted that I eat with the family, at least one meal a day. Once she took great pride in preparing a special meal for me—fish and sweet potatoes—which tasted better to me than anything I had ever eaten. And when I would come into the compound, she would send Iba to sweep out a space beneath the acacia tree and spread the mat, preparing a place for me in the heart of the family. If there were still embers on the fire, she would send for Gunpowder tea and mint—in order to prepare the syrupy Arabic tea that accompanied all gatherings and conversations. And she would sing of my family, of the parents that had raised me, of the ancestors that she felt spoke through me. It was really a cross between singing and speaking, long and drawn-out like poetry, with inflections and shape in the lines. As she poured the tea from cup to cup in order to create the thick froth that marks a good cup, she rocked back and forth, child strapped to that strong back.

And Abdou and the other children sat round in the intense still heat of early evening.

Of all the children, why was it Iba, the oldest and strongest, who got malaria?

I hadn't been to the Diop compound for a few days. It was exam period, and I was busy with the high school entrance test that I administered in the next town. I got back to my village late one night after a long and dusty ride on a bush taxi that I had spent all afternoon waiting for in the company of camels.

I stopped by the Diop compound. It was quiet. I noticed the pot of boiled herbs near the smoking fire. Then I could hear the labored breathing and the moaning. Maïmouna came up, greeted me curtly, and grabbed my hand and pulled me into the windowless shack. "Can you give him something? It's malaria," she said in broken French. Iba lay on the mat, his head swathed in dripping herbs. Beads and *gris-gris*—traditional cures—were attached to his arms and head. What I'll never forget is the milky color and empty expression of those eyes. I ran for my house and the medicine supply.

There was even enough time for me to develop a little righteous indignation. The villagers would turn to western remedies (or western aid) only when their own systems failed, and by then it was often too late. I had told Abdou time and again to keep his kids on malaria prophylaxis—I would supply the medication—to avoid such problems. But now the disease had hit, there was no time.

"Half a tablet now, the other half tomorrow." I didn't stay to watch them wash the tablet down with fetid water.

The dawn came silently, brilliantly lighting all things in its progress. I was outside on the mat that, nightly, I unfurled underneath my Peace Corps-issue mosquito net strung between two neem trees. No chance of rain, not here—just a horizon illuminated only by stars, no false incandescence from lamps. I got up and lighted my little gas stove so that I could make my morning instant coffee. I would get to the Diops as soon as I finished breakfast.

People were walking in the streets, more people than usual for this time of day—men in their fez hats, dressed in their boubous. But this wasn't Friday, not the holy day. And morning prayer was already over: no one could be heading to the mosque after the prayer call.

I went out to see for myself. There, in front of the Diop compound, a carpet of mats reached out into the sandy street. People were seated here and there, pulling on their chaplets, saying little. New arrivals in small groups would step inside the compound for a few moments then return out front to greet the others and join them on the mats. It was the villagers' way of responding to a death in their community

So, it happened. I remembered I was a stranger to this village and walked back to my home to cry, apart and alone. He was just a kid; he shouldn't have died. Then I put on my good school clothes, practiced the correct pronunciation of the Arabic words of condolence, and headed back to take my place in front of my family's compound.

Chapter Two
Grass

Socio-biologists talk about the "savannah syndrome," a sort of genetic blueprinting that predisposes people to prefer landscapes that feature an ocean of short grasses interrupted by occasional islands of vertical trees. So, the thinking goes, people automatically associate a landscape of short grass and singular trees with identifiable and calming home spaces. So it may be that we atavistically trace our feelings of home and home spaces back to aboriginal African ancestors—despite the varied terrains of our present lives. The savannah scape of seasonal grass and rugged, rare trees has become, according to the theory, imprinted on human psychology and, more important, planted inside the human genome. The savannah is thus the original and archetypal eden, despite claims of Jews or Christians.

It is not hard to imagine that this theory is true when you stand on the savannah at the beginning of the season of rains. In my case, it was the Sahel region of West Africa, not the more well-known Olduvai Gorge in what is now called Tanzania. I had been doing some research in Senegal, and I planned to visit the home village of my friend Maalik, in the North of the country. Propitiously enough, both my travel plans and the rainy season were running late that year, 1998.

An August visit to the North would usually have taken me through impassable muddy troughs that during the long dry season serve quite well as roads that crisscross this thinly-populated stretch of sandy land punctuated by scrubby trees and small baobabs. For those of us used to four seasons and precipitation in all months of the year, the shift to wet-and-dry seasons is disconcerting. Here, the sun beats hot and impossibly dry for nine months of the year, and by February or March most of the spiny bushes have exfoliated while the wind burning down from the Sahara blows the sandy soil into plates of food and the most unwanted places. There is no hint of anything alive in the ground, only the warning thorns or the clutching offerings of a few rampant plants, long since browned and   desiccated.   As   the   season   of   rains   approaches,   the   relative

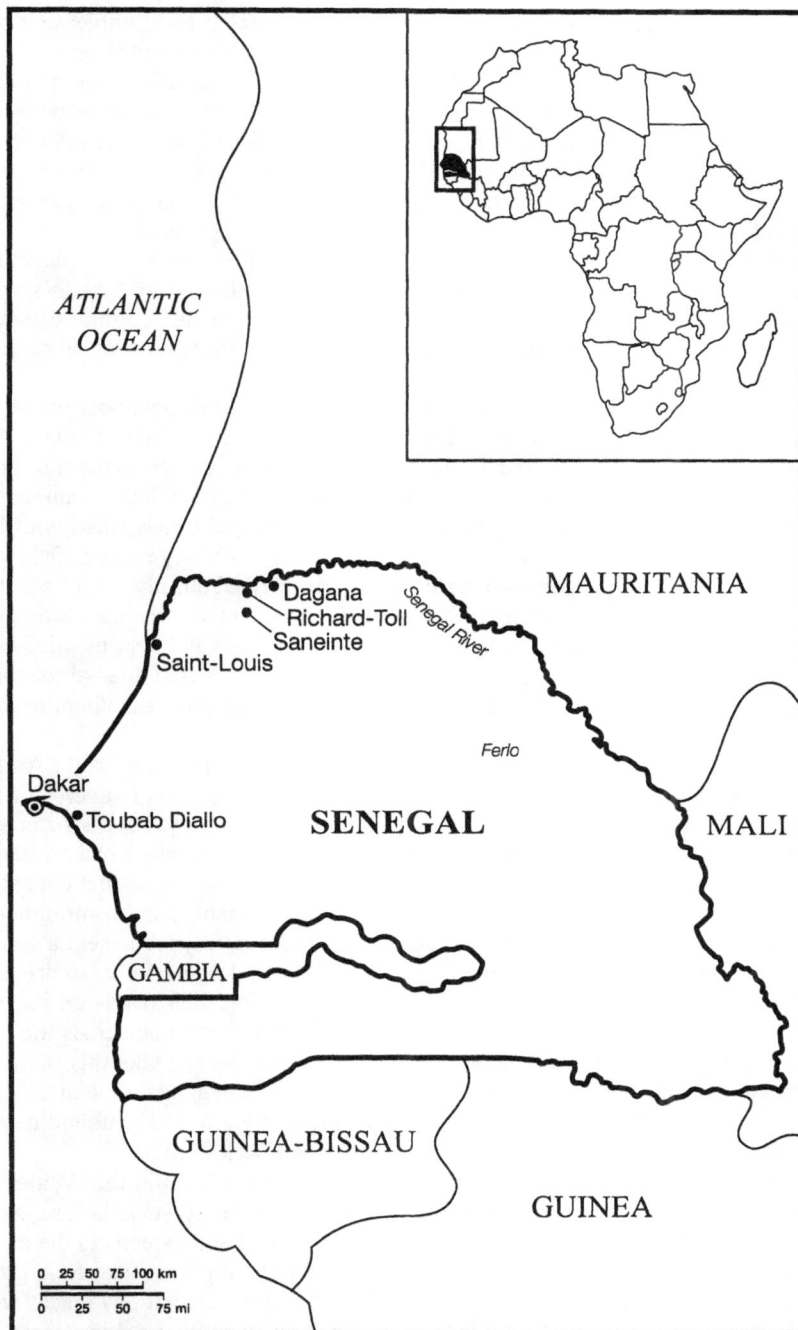

humidity increases along with the temperature to make a most unpleasant preamble to the limited deluges that must water the region for an entire year.

But the rains arrived late in 1998. Drifting in great clouds up from the Gulf of Guinea, they were set back, perhaps, by the turmoil in Sierra Leone or by the coup d'état in Guinea Bissau. Or perhaps La Niña affected more than American weather patterns that year. Most likely, the fickle monsoon clouds spent themselves long before they reached Senegal on the edge of that hot huge desert. Irrespective of politics or other human schedules, the rains came late.

We too were delayed—by our decision to stop in St. Louis, the ancient colonial city on the coast. We had to pay a visit to the family of Maalik's wife, who had stayed behind in New York City at an unimaginable cultural distance. We should have known, however, that in Africa you can never drop in on people.

No sooner had we arrived than the women of the family set about preparing a special meal for us. Maalik and I were taken to meet all the adults in the household at the time—around 15 people; then we were led across town to greet a distantly-related uncle and his family. Several hours after our unannounced arrival, the entire household gathered round large enamel bowls filled with fragrant *cheb oo jen*—rice cooked in a tomato base with vegetables, fish, and plenty of habañero peppers—made in our honor. Seynabou, my friend's sister-in-law, took special care of us: to the meal she contributed *boulettes*, little nuggets of highly-seasoned fish; she found fans for us to use and kept us plied with cool water. Then, after the unexpected lunch, she prepared tea—three little glasses of bitter-sweet frothy brew that takes hours to prepare and about as long to sip.

Late in the afternoon we finally made it outside to the car, a bright American Jeep, with an entourage of about a half a dozen kids and several of the adults, including Seynabou. We talked more—about how Seynabou's sister was managing in New York, about where we were going, about why I had chosen to visit Senegal. Then we began the long and complicated exchanges that constitute leave-taking, an important gesture that reaffirms relationships and commitments. As the ritual statement of goodbye began to wind down, Seynabou sent a couple of the kids to the corner store to get bottles of Coke and Fanta for us to drink on the way. The other kids climbed inside the car, rubbing their hands on its slippery brown interior. The voice of the muezzin from the mosque across the way called out salaam to the neighborhood, but my friend did not take this occasion to pray. We accepted the drinks, expressed our thanks again, then slipped through dirty puddles as we made our way to the single paved road and east to the interior of the country, up the Senegal River and back in time.

With my friend's car we made good time. I had not been in the Waalo, the region of the river, since a dam had been built more than 10 years before. Now, where the road comes close to the river, a bright green band extends to the north. Channels and canals siphon the water away from the river and make for a green mosaic that, at times, reaches many miles from the river. Only a few places were still dry and dusty, despite the arrival of the rainy season. Looking closely I could see the thin layer of salt that lay like an overgrazing of the thin grass cover.

Yet by and large the land seemed so productive. Fields of sugar cane stood tall and green, occasional palms broke the nearly flat horizon, patches of vegetables luxuriated in private plots. The sun began to drop behind us as we approached Richard Toll, the town where we would turn south towards Maalik's village, on sandy tracks that figure on no maps.

How strange it was to travel that flat country at night, our headlights beaming on groups of people walking back to their home villages, surprising the occasional horse and buggy, more likely illuminating a sleeping baobab tree on its solitary watch of the quiet land or scaring up an unlikely hare that had managed to survive the long dry season now munching on the luxuriant grass. In these regions where not much more than 10 inches of rain falls in a given year, even the baobabs are small, yet they tower over the other vegetation, scrubby trees and spiny shrubs, spaced at strangely wide intervals, the regularity of which almost suggests some rationalizing human intervention.

But the real vision was the grass, the unexpected carpet of green that, in the artificial light of the headlamps, appeared richer than any cash crop. A thin layer of brilliant light green extended as far as I could see, right up to the edges of the makeshift road. About a foot high at his point—after a rain or two—the grass spread unbroken and uniform like some fantastical green wave where, only days, before, the ground was dead and brown. Then, like great green shelters, trees reached out and up from the land floor, never in woody thickets, but all spread about to maximize the limited water supply and interrupt the grass expanse. Occasionally a stocky baobab, whose bole stores up water from the few profligate rains of the summer, but more often less dramatic plants—the little spiny bush the Wolof people call *sump*, which yields bitter but edible fruit and leaves; the non-deciduous leafy *pooftan*, which exudes a milky sap and which, when burned, makes a sweet-smelling incense-like smoke that wafts around the villages here at night—populate these plains suddenly sprung green, relieved to be brought to life in the annual inundation. And the green grass will feed the goats and sheep (once antelope and elephant) weakened by months of nomadic foraging, which in turn will feed the villagers, many of whom now spend the long dry months looking for work in the unnatural cities.

The word *grass* shares its Indo-Aryan roots with the words *grain*, *green*, and *grow*. The linguistic connections of grass thus reflect its importance as both cultivated food and cultural concept. Known at least to biologists is the fact that 70% of the world's agricultural land is given over to the growing of crop grasses—wheat, rye, oats, and corn among others—that feed the world's people. What has contributed to the resilience of grass plants is that they grow from the base of the plant, not a main stem, and are hence not harmed by grazing, mowing, or the effects of fire, which is a recurrent threat in savannah climates. Durable and ubiquitous grasses flourish throughout the world; grasses please both the eye and the palette.

None of this etymological and agricultural information was available to me as I trekked across the Senegal savannah in 1998, however. Nor could I have been aware that, at that moment, Fulani herdsmen were leading their flocks of sheep and goats north and east, following the monsoon rains and the spread of the sea of green grass in the Sahel as the herdsmen and their herds flee from population centers. I did know that the villagers would soon plant fields of millet in concentric circles extending outward from the village center. Millet, a form of grass, grows well in the sandy soil and the uncertain rainfall of this part of the Sahel; in the wetter southern portion of the country, the Senegalese plant its botanical cousin, rice. Grass feeds both human and animal populations here.

In the village we slept outside, and early the first morning we were awakened by a storm. From the southwest, winds blew strong; the villagers' huts and palisade fences shuddered. Finally the rain came in horizontal sheets, pooling up and then disappearing into the sieve-like soil. In that sudden fierce storm I felt strangely vulnerable in that little collection of huts on that expanse of flat land surrounded by grassy bush and no sizable trees. Yet I also felt an ineffable closeness to that land, as if it had been a place I had known all my life. At that moment I was struck by the beauty of the village to which I felt a calming emotional connection. Maybe it was a sudden onset of the savannah syndrome, but this was not my first acquaintance with grass nor with quiet rural spaces. As a good midwestern boy, I had grown up mowing—and hating—lawns, and I spent my first ten (and happy) years living on a dysfunctional farm in northern Ohio. No, my affection for the village in its isolated association with encompassing grass was real, and it was strong. It felt like home.

Our plans changed, and we had to leave the village the following day. We began the leave-taking early so that we could make the rounds of everyone in the village. As we were about to go, one of the old men came forward, took us aside, and squatted down on the sand not far from the Jeep; we knew to do the same. Chanting suras from the Koran, he drew ceremoniously in the sand, spat in his hands then erased the drawings. He repeated this action several times. Then he invited Maalik and me to touch the soil ourselves. We did so. He took my hands—dirt and sand stuck to my fingers—in his own and vigorously shook them. He did the same with Maalik. I see now that this was a gesture that announced our taking leave of both the people and the place. Maalik and I got into the Jeep and drove off with kids chasing us.

Though we had been in the village a short time, I noticed that, in the tracks the Jeep had left a few days before, green grass had already sprouted.

Chapter Three
Naming the Faith

From the enclosed space of my mud-walled hut in arid northern Senegal I could visualize Père de Foucauld in his monastic digs miles north into the intense heat of the Sahara and southern Algeria. My Catholic friends had shown me découpage pictures of Foucauld, gaunt in his limp cassock but with an expression of deep peace. I was intrigued and read the slim French biography: how he was born into fabulous wealth and spent the rest of his life getting away from money and the false values that the worship of money engenders; how he lived several lives, first as a profligate (the French sounds better here—*débauché*), then a cavalry officer in the Sahara.

It was in the Sahara that he was hooked: maybe his life of aristocratic ease seemed abjectly absurd as he roamed through the rocky oceans of the western Sahara, sharing its formidable spaces with rare Tuareg and Fulani nomads as brilliant European birds flew overhead, not stopping until they had reached green, tropical gardens far to the south. Unlike the birds, he stayed.

Earlier in his life, Charles Eugène de Foucauld had rejected everything he had and everything he had been and joined the austere Trappist monastery at Notre Dame des Neiges, Our Lady of the Snow, a path not too different from that taken by Thomas Merton in the 1950s. Yet even the Trappists were not severe enough for Foucauld, and in 1901 he left France to take up life as a hermit in the Sahara. Around 1905 he found a place as remote and physically rigorous as any—a skimpy oasis, Tamanrasset, near the Ahaggar Mountains. Summer month highs of 120 degrees or more; freezing temperatures in the unexpected winter. The map of northern Africa is void of place names, though most maps I've checked include a dot and the word *Tamanrasset* in the midst of other foreign words—*wadi, erg, aïr*. A place where physical comfort is reduced to a minimum, a place for the soul to grow.

The biography provides a daguerreotype photo of Foucauld, surrounded by a field of rocks, kneeling before an open-air altar, also of stone. The biography goes on to say that Foucauld believed that it was necessary to live the life of the poor in order to understand what is most precious and most truly human about life. Though he lived alone—no other brothers joined him in community—Foucauld was a well-known local legend and had enough interaction with Tuareg people to compile a Tuareg-French dictionary. The biographer notes that his patient, listening wisdom earned him the title *Christian marabout* among the settled people.

For the Muslims of this part of Africa a marabout is both religious leader and magician. I imagine that, for the Tuareg, the magic consisted in the monk's coming out of the northern sand—like a mirage—to live among people not his own, make few or no demands of others, leave open the door to his simple home and life of devotion. The Tuareg knew a wise man when they saw one. They gave him a name.

And there I was, 21 years old and a Peace Corps volunteer teaching English to people for whom America was as immaterial as wealth. One of my students, Moctar Bousso, asked if I might want to spend my summer recess with him in his village in the interior of Senegal, part of the Ferlo desert. Moctar was an excellent student, quiet and serious; he was widely regarded as wise beyond his years (he must have been about 20 at the time), a devout Muslim. During the academic year he lived with some relatives in Dagana, our dusty riverine town, so that he could attend the only secondary school for a couple hundred miles around, the lycée where I worked. I had not figured out what I would do during the four-month summer recess, so Moctar's invitation could not have come at a better time. A chance for me to live with a family. There would be work for me to do: we planned that I would work with him in the family fields during the day, teach French to villagers in the evenings. In June I left my river town and the lycée, taking my bag of clothes and map of Africa with me.

I so much wanted to be part of life in Saneinte, Moctar's village. His people had worked the thin soil here for years, always waiting patiently for unpredictable summer rain, their livelihood tied to the price of peanuts and beans. I moved into one of the empty huts inside his family's compound, a collection of about seven huts outlined by a flimsy millet-stalk fence that kept out goats and neighbors' eyes. Square and small, with hard-packed dirt floors and mud-daubed walls under a roof of millet thatch, the hut could quickly cool after a day of torrid heat and keep me out of the rare summer downpours. It was a sanctuary.

Though newly arrived from town, I took part in the first planting in early June. Millet, peanuts, sweet potatoes—planted in little patches that crisscrossed the flat sandy expanse, broken only by occasional baobabs, those stout trees that look crazily uprooted, carrying enormous racks of barren limbs much of the year.

In the first-light moments of that first day, most of the village had assembled underneath the single kapok tree that shaded the small public space—the palaver tree—before heading out to the fields that stretched in great rings from the center of the village of 50 or 60 huts. Moctar sat with members of his immediate family off to the side on a large woven mat spread across the sand. He was dressed in a T-shirt stamped with the bold green letters of the words *Ohio Uni-*

versity and in purple pants two sizes too big—the final destination of some Goodwill donation from America. He had a bad eye; it sat motionless in the socket, never moving to help its mate focus or discern. Moctar got up from the mat so that he could address the villagers. He spoke in the local language Wolof about the land and its connection to the people. How easily he spoke in a low yet commanding voice. Then he pronounced some words in Arabic, a blessing for the work about to begin. I was amazed that the important task of addressing the villagers was assigned to Moctar, more my mentor than my student.

In the fields I worked next to his family members, pushing the *gop* in, then pulling it back, creating a small drill in the sand with this flattened hoe. It was only the men at first; then, near 9 o'clock the women came, carrying large enamel bowls on their heads, which where swathed in bright scarves. They sang as they swayed along the path, children strapped to their backs. We could hear them before they appeared before us, bearing breakfast. Rice cooked with dried fish in pieces and a few beans. It was, after all, the end of the dry season, and there was almost nothing left in the larder. As we ate in silence I started to pick out the cooked maggots from my portion but stopped myself. I felt it would appear rude.

I worked in the fields most mornings. How strange it must have seemed to have a white visitor helping. Once, a group of Fulani passed through with their herd of skinny goats. One man pointed excitedly at me as I stood up and wiped the sweat from my forehead in the 110-degree heat. The others were nonchalant but kept to the distant side of the field as they passed, their eyes never leaving me. They may still today tell tales of the apparition.

For the first two weeks I spent the afternoons getting ready for the French language class that I held at night. I had found an abandoned building just outside the village. It had been a primary school, and Moctar had been the star pupil in the early days. But the teacher quit. Left for good. As far as anyone knew, the government didn't even know that there was no longer a school. Like so many other things, the school collapsed silently, and the villagers returned to their lives as sand invaded the windowless building and roaches took up residence.

I decided I would clean up the building and asked the women for a broom. I couldn't understand the Wolof they were speaking, and no one could translate it into French for me. Something about dust. I spent a day sweeping up great clouds of long-dormant dust. That day was followed by a week of sleepless nights and long days, as I scratched at the minute blood-red bugs that crawled all over my body. Finally, I bought kerosene from a neighbor and doused myself and the little buggers. I was cured.

Three weeks after my arrival in Saneinte I opened the school. A number of villagers showed up, and we practiced counting in French and exchanging simple questions and answers: *Where do you live? What is your family name? How much do you want? How much does this cost?* They were all willing to learn the colonial language, which they needed in the selling of their crops in the towns at the end of the season. I'll never forget the sound of those classes. We had hung hurricane lamps around the empty building, and the drone of the insects sucked into the shine almost drowned out our human voices.

The lessons went quickly. We looked at the literacy manuals the French embassy provided—pictures of earthen water jugs and the letter C (for *canari*); a few pages later a drawing of the gop; later still, a sketch of healthy millet fields illustrating the letter M for *mil*. A period of questions and answers and counting practice completed our session of an hour or so: we had no more energy for words or thought. After working all day in the sun, everyone was tired. Besides, we didn't want to be late for the final prayer call, prelude to sleep.

It was up with the muezzin early early every morning, then to the fields. Sometimes in the morning I'd put up my gop and take a walk in the quiet calm of the savannah. There, flowers grew inadvertently, despite the lack of rain and the absolute porosity of the soil. There is a wild narcissus, whose petals are long and narrow, unlike its hybrid relatives. Watermelons grow wild, and the villagers could count on a refreshing drink on the most arid of days if they came across watermelons. Not the sweet pink kinds that we know, but white and wet. And the thorny bush called *sump*, which yields sweetish berries at the end of the brief period of rains. And of course the magnificent baobabs, marker of Sahelian regions. Enormous, bloated, cantankerous inhabitants of the bush whose leaves anticipate the rain and appear mysteriously in the midst of the driest days of the dry season. Villagers eat the acrid leaves and the chalky inside of the seed pods—both excellent sources of calcium in a land where, according to Western accounts, nutrition is considered naturally poor.

In July the wind changed, shifting to a southerly flow from the Sahara.

After a promising beginning, the rainy season abruptly stopped. At first the millet continued to grow, as if nourished by the sand and insufferable heat. But no rain. And, to make matters worse, the sky taunted us each afternoons with gatherings and collisions of purple clouds. Sweltering heat but no rain. Week after week of wetless days and nights. First the millet stalks stopped growing, then they began to sag in the long afternoon sun, its rays striking us almost from the vertical. Insects made strident cries into the night hours.

Yet Moctar prayed each day the five prayers, touching his forehead to the sand in respect for the earth and for his final earthly home. He never missed the five prayers, whether in his family compound or in the middle of the tessellated fields. Already he had been given the name *El Hadj*, the one who has made the pilgrimage to Mecca. Moctar hadn't been to Mecca, of course, but the title was a sign of the villagers' great respect for him and for his knowledge of the Koran. His knowledge was sufficient for Moctar to be a Koranic teacher, and when he wasn't working in the fields, he sat on the ground in his compound under a small acacia tree surrounded by children, who clutched small wooden slates and scratched out time and again the beautiful Arabic script of the Koran with their quill pens as they chanted, together and aloud. I listened from my hut—Moctar's call, the students' response, back and forth, again and again. Then the scratching of goose quill on the soft wood, right to left, in the language that joins alphabet and art. I could not tell how many suras were sung that summer; but the language, like incense from a swaying censer, drifted across the compound mystically, invitingly.

Late in August the crickets came—great black clouds from the Sahara. What could they have been feeding on up there in that rocky wasteland? Each arrival of an insect cloud was preceded by a baleful blast of the especially hot, dry wind, the harmattan. Some of the millet had managed to tassel in the drought, but those sentinel heads were easy targets for the insects. They devoured what little had come to seed, leaving broken stalks behind as they pillaged south. The villagers made little commentary as they kept up their husbandry of broken crops.

Family larders were even more depleted. And yet Moctar gave a portion of his every meal to the beggars that made the rounds of the village. I watched him day after day as he would reach for a hollowed-out gourd and scoop out gloppy rice or grainy millet. The beggars would huddle in groups just outside the main gate to the concession, uttering a ritual request, shuffling in the sand. They always looked the same to me: ageless, dressed in filthy bits of rags, barefoot, expressionless. And Moctar would divide up the food into the tin cans the beggars held out to him. *Thank you, El Hadj.* Islam enjoins its practitioners to give alms: no matter how bad things are, there is always someone for whom things are worse. I couldn't help thinking how, in countries where capitalism motivates social activity, people with so much more give so much less.

August passed, and it was time for the fasting month of Ramadan to begin. Moctar explained that villagers were not permitted to swallow anything from sun-up to sunset—for the entire month. He told me that discipline shapes devotion. I tried my own fast and made it through one day, at the end of which I was parched and exhausted—no more for me. Yet the villagers kept up their trek to the fields each morning, spitting out the liquid that accumulated in their mouths as they worked, in keeping with the Koranic teaching. The women who had stayed behind prepared special drinks and foods for the meal that took place just as the sun sank behind the baobabs to the west. This went on for the entire circuit of the moon. Evenings, no one could talk much; everyone sat exhausted on mats stretched out in front of the dying cooking fires. Occasionally someone would toss a handful of incense on the coals, and thick, exotic smoke would ooze out and waft around, a small balm for the pain of those long dry days.

Physically and emotionally tired, I had long before given up my gop and the daily jaunt into the fields, yet Moctar went each day. He would return as the sun reached its cruelest height. Greater fatigue in a person I have never seen. So tired he had to gather all remaining strength simply to return my greetings, yet he never avoided me, always smiled quietly in my presence, asked after my family members he could never know. I never asked him but always wondered: *Why do you continue? Is this how your god answers your prayers, responds to your obedience? Is this how your god cares for you?*

Some relief: the rains picked up again. And the sheath of grass that had once covered the sand reappeared, even more gloriously green. The peanuts and the sweet potatoes, lovers of drought, would be all right. There was even hope for the shorter type of millet, the fonio. Here and there, pools of muddy water formed in the depressions. The hoofed prints of Fulani animals made rings around the temporary lakes. And the mosquitoes laid their eggs.

Malaria came with those mosquitoes. It starts as a violent headache accompanied by the chills and can kill people already overworked and undernourished. I had kept up my prophylaxis and, before coming, had illegally raided the Peace Corps doctor's drug keep to get Aralen for the villagers to use if things got bad. So, during that hot Ramadan, I became a human dispensary, doling out drugs. No one in the village died from malaria, at least not that summer.

But I can still hear the moaning. By September the late afternoons were so hot that stretching out under a tree was about the only thing I could do. Sweat poured off my reddened face so generously that reading became a book bath. The late-afternoon prayer call *Takusan* would usually find me spread out on a mat, staring up into the kapok tree in the village center, listening to village sounds—the pounding of the mortars and pestles, the soughing of the acacias in the slight breeze. And the quiet moaning through thatched walls.

We nursed Moctar through his fever, making regular runs to the single well that served two entire villages, changing the wetted rags that we placed across his gentle head. For three days he lay on the dirt floor of his hut unaware of our names, maybe even of our human presence. It may have been the only time he missed his prayers, or did not actively give to the poor, or did not profess his faith to his students and to the village community.

For me that was the final straw. I walked around with a kind of numb emptiness. *What kind of god watches while the most faithful followers sicken, some die? What kind of god withholds rain, sends vermin and hot winds, when the people are already neither wealthy nor proud? What kind of god rewards prayer and fasting with sickness and starvation?* I was filled with a mute, righteous indignation: life for these people should be better.

My summer break spend with Moctar had turned out unexpectedly. I'm sure that it was I who learned the most that summer. After all, I knew so little about local life. The summer taught me that real life is *only* local.

By the end of September, only two or three people still came to the night classes, but I wasn't surprised: the summer had been long, hot, and very hard. The French lessons petered out. Moctar's health improved, though he never really recovered his strength and was left with a persistent cough. Just before the millet was to be harvested, he and I hopped onto a passing truck that was carrying manioc to Dagana. The lycée would reopen in October; we needed to get back.

Funny that the young man whose learning and living I so respected, even revered, was my own student. El Hadj Moctar Bousso. Sometimes I would catch myself saying his name aloud, *El Hadj Moctar Bousso*, trying in my delivery to achieve the rhythm and reverence that the villagers came by naturally. In the village, all names are known. And your name tells who you are, who your parents are, and who, likely, your children will become. Though the villagers could not know my parents or the children who came years later, they felt that they knew me: someone who willingly came from another world to live and work in a village in the inhospitable savannah. They gave me the name *Baba Touré*. My other name.

***

It took me years to come to terms with events of that summer in the Sahel. It took me years to stop cursing gods and the faith they inspire in people. It took me years to realize that, in part, life is precious because it is fragile. And, as humans, we are strengthened by good work and deepened by pain. The villagers worked hard and were visited with much pain.

Fifteen years later I got another chance to go to Africa, this time as a lecturer in American literature in Madagascar—*my* work. On the way back from my first year I arranged a trip through West Africa and back to Moctar's village. It had taken me months to summon up the courage to return, for the intervening years had been cruel—my own lessons in pain.

In my Peace Corps days there had been four of us friends at the lycée in the river town: Moctar; Tidiane Diop—the young, dreamy poet I called *Spacebird*; Mohammed, a light-skinned Mauritanian; and me. Of the four, I was the only one yet alive, though my friends were all younger than I. Tidiane had died from tuberculosis about three years after we parted; he had not finished his high school education. Mohammed had left for Mauritania, where he had brilliantly finished his high school and undergraduate studies, only to die from malaria just a couple of months out of school. And El Hadj Moctar Bousso, who died as he would have wanted—in his village, in the midst of his people, in 1985. The accounts of his death make mention of no known disease or curable illness. The villagers later told me that he got thinner and thinner, the cough regularly racked his body, and he was taken from the capital city Dakar back to Saneinte where he died quietly one December day.

As the bush-taxi scampered across the Sahel sand, I wondered how much the village would have changed in the years since my first visit. As we approached, I was surprised to find Saneinte so full of life. I should have noticed that the tire tracks through the sand were well-worn. I should have noticed that the fields reached even more deeply out into the savannah. I should have known that the pulse of life here would still be strong. But I never imagined that my return would feel like a homecoming.

Saneinte was still a collection of 60 or so huts. The millet-stalk fences still swung in irregular circles around the compounds. The tall kapok still stood, center of the village and reminder of a wetter, greener past when the fringes of the Sahara got regular rains. The school building still cowered on the edge of the village, its roof now completely gone. Occasional green from private patches of squash and beans punctuated the stretches of sand tight near the concessions. Some thatch huts had been replaced by red-earth banco bricks, and someone—the villagers thought it was the Japanese—had come in and built a latrine.

And the village sounds were familiar as a friend's voice. The women pounding the millet in their big wooden mortars and clapping their hands in unison as they let go of the pestles just before the descent back into the wooden mortars. Goats and sheep, tethered to thorn bushes and trees, wailing. The continuous strain of the village pump that creaked as water was brought up and sent crashing into the enamel pans that the villagers had assembled as catch-basins. The muezzin's chant—Takusan prayer time—calling all people from work or lay to turn inward, touch the ground, offer foreign words of supplication, words long since appropriated into the human spiritual vocabulary. *Allahu akbar. Allahu akbar. Bismillah rabbil alamin.*

The bush taxi slid to a stop in the village center. I thought of El Hadj Moctar Bousso. How he had known that humans need to be attached to a place. How he had known that people need to remind themselves that they live on the earth and with the earth. How he had known that humans need to work for themselves but think always of others. How he had known that people cling to words when there is not sure knowledge for them to reach toward. I was wiping tears away from my eyes as the dust settled and the car door opened.

"*Asalaam alaikum, Baba Touré*," the villagers said, by way of greeting. They had not forgotten my name.

***

Saneinte does not appear on any map of Africa that I have seen. In the map of my mind it is the place where my spirit was formed.

Charles Eugène de Foucauld was first formed at Notre Dame des Neiges. Curiously, Notre Dame des Neiges is not located atop some craggy alpine peak staring down on cascades or across at snowy fields: Foucauld found this monastic community in Nazareth, the biblical town, and there he began his life of increasing asceticism. Imagine Mary caring for her infant in the midst of some freak snowstorm, as the white weight bends low the fronds of the shocked date palm or the olives shudder to shake off icy accumulations. Imagine the young aristocrat shunning comfort in search of a spiritual winter. Asceticism: accepting physical hardship as an assignment, which conditions the body and frees the spirit.

Thomas Merton too sought hardship—ironically, in the green plenty of Middle America. After giving up an active social and intellectual life as a student of Columbia University, he boarded a train headed for the Trappist monastery in Gethsemani, Kentucky. Even at this early age he must have understood Gandhi's observation that there can be no worship without sacrifice. The sacrifice began: long days of physical work and intervening quiet, minimal attention to human wants, long stretches of silence with no human interlocution—emotional winter. The regime was still not austere enough: Merton later asked for further remove, greater silence, increased discomfort. The brothers built him a hut—cinder-block and square—apart from the monastic buildings.

For me there is an important paradox here: *How can separating yourself from other people ever serve to increase your understanding of the human condition?*

How the two monks perished may serve as a response to this question. Despite his removal from day-to-day social activities, Merton was, to the end, deeply involved in the activities of people, and, in particular, the ecumenical movement. In 1970 he left his concrete cell for Bangkok, where a gathering of religious leaders from around the world was taking place, a sort of spiritual summit meeting. It was at this meeting that Merton died, electrocuted as he jimmied with the faulty wiring of his hotel room fan. At a meeting where he was to deliver a talk, where people waited to hear his wisdom. The world knew of this reclusive, sedentary monk from rural Kentucky.

In 1916 the first rumblings of the Great War in Europe could not have been heard in Tamanrasset despite Europe's colonial grasp on much of Africa. But a war of its own was taking place in the oasis: marauders attacked the town, killing, among others, a white outsider whom the local people called *Christian marabout*. Today, small groups of selfless men and women live together in the poorest neighborhoods of cities throughout the world. Their vows are similar: to live among poor people, do what the poor people of that region do, share what they have with neighbors, sacrifice their self-interest as a means of devotion to God and God's people. Those men and women look to Père de Foucauld, the Christian marabout, for inspiration and hope.

And I too have learned from an unlikely master—the young Senegalese Muslim with a bad eye, El Hadj Moctar Bousso. He taught me that spiritual growth begins when we work to reduce material want. He taught me that wisdom starts with a commitment to a people and a place. I now know that such spiritual lessons are good for us—because of, not despite, the privation. They help us to know and name our own faith.

Chapter Four
Toubab Diallo

As much love as I have for certain villages in Senegal, I have no love at all for Dakar, the capital and largest city. Dakar would be considered modern by most western standards: there are high-rise buildings with views of the Atlantic, attractive boutiques and cafés filled with high-priced imported goods, posh residential districts where large trees spread their shade over villas and fences support fragrant and irrigated jasmine and allamanda vines. Yet it is in Dakar—as in all African cities that I have visited—where the gross inequities of living standards are most clearly seen and where western life-styles most clearly clash with African traditions. On my way into Africa I wish I could bypass Dakar and land without the hassle of customs somewhere inside the country, away from the ugly noise and social squalor of the city.

But the airport lies just north of Dakar, and most roads take you through the city. Most guide books encourage visitors to stop for lunch or a drink at one of Dakar's lovely cafés. But you need to think twice about sitting outside. The minute you sit down, from just outside the enclosure beggars will gather round you, thrusting fists of half-formed fingers into your sight as you try to sip your beer or cool tropical drink. If the management has hired a boy or two to beat the beggars off (a practice which may itself compromise your comfort), then you can be sure that the mass of vendors and street people will lay in wait just outside the reach of the boys' batons, ready to attach themselves like leeches to you as you set foot on the street. Even the most steely-eyed New Yorker would have trouble fending off these insistent mendicants. They have nothing to lose and plenty to gain in a country where many people make not much more than a dollar a day.

Like most African cities, the population of Dakar has exploded in the last decades of the twentieth century, and the large number of relative newcomers are pretty much crammed into the limited confines of the colonial city. Dakar's narrow streets were never designed for this volume of traffic—gargantuan SUV's (that denote the wealthiest of the locals or the toubabs, foreign and white), ancient Peugeots and Renaults, *cars-rapides* (something like pick-up trucks for passengers), mopeds (the French call them *mobylettes*), donkey carts, bicycles, and throngs of pedestrians. So many people, a small place, few jobs—a bad combination. Even among African cities, Dakar has a reputation as a place where poverty is particularly aggressive.

Actually, the problem is that local people have learned the lessons of capitalism too well. Everything is up for sale. You never need to ask to see a product: it will surely appear before your eyes before long. On my last visit, the most prevalent item for sale was small packages of Kleenex; they were thrust through open car windows as we waited at street lights. You quickly learn to dread the inevitable traffic jams. The instant you are immobilized, a small army of sellers descends onto your vehicle, sometimes fighting each other off for the chance to hawk contraband Kleenex or imitation American cigarettes. On a corner, a woman sits behind a mountain of used clothing (the future economic life of Goodwill donations perhaps) participating in what the Wolof call *fook ee jy,* "shake and sell." The locals have learned too well the meaning of salesmanship: everything can be sold, and everybody can be hustled.

How I prefer life in the village. It is hard to imagine that this could be the same country, these the same people.

My friend Maalik has a home just south of Dakar; it faces out onto the ocean and sits just above the village of Toubab Diallo. When Maalik is away on business, our friend Vieux watches over the place, watering the young coconut palms in the enclosed yard. In 1998 I spent several weeks with Vieux and Maalik; I was introduced to Toubab Diallo then.

Arriving late after a day spent fighting off the city, Maalik and I realize that we have no food for dinner and decide to see what the day's catch has brought into Toubab Diallo. We leave Maalik's stone hut on the dry, rocky cliff that looks 30 feet or so down to the Atlantic Ocean. Though the land along the sea has been parceled out for some distance (the Germans and the Italians have bought large tracts that will be developed as exclusive vacation resorts catering to tourists and wealthier Africans), there is no easy access to the beach or to the village of Toubab Diallo. So we have to sidle down the embankment, following paths that skirt the fields of bubbly basalt rock shot blood red in the chasmic blast that formed this land mass that is still running from the Americas.

The western sky shifts from red to dark as the day withdraws. We can hear the sounds of the fishing boats (*pirogues* in French; *gal* in Wolof) as they ride the waves into the beach. Villagers wade into the surf and grab the shallow boats in order to guide them to their resting place on the beach. At this moment, the beach has become the village. All those thatched huts and mud houses clinging to the cliff or perched just beyond the cliff's jutting edge—all these homes are dark and quiet.

The beach, however, is alive. It isn't a huge beach, maybe 75 feet at its widest, maybe a couple of hundred feet in length. But the rocky ledges give way, bend low to the sea at this point, and the dry clays of the highlands shift to the clean smooth sand of the beach.

Groups of boys dart around kicking and chasing a beat-up soccer ball. Their heads are shaved and smudged with mercurochrome where the razor has nicked them. Younger kids sit in sand; others crawl. From time to time, an adult will sit them up, move them from the encroaching surf, or lift and cuddle them. My friend Vieux points to an older man playing with a baby. He wears the blue boubou and the signs of age. He sits tickling somebody's child; the child laughs, braced in the man's bony hand. This beach is baby sitter and playground for the village; all adults accept the responsibility for attending to all children who happen to be near them.

But the ultimate focus is the boats, and the human and fish cargo that they carry. The villagers spend two days at a time on these small craft—15 feet long at most—two days in the full sun and strong surf chasing fish in these waters. As the gal approach the beach, villagers run to meet them—aging men in their long boubous and red fez hats; women in their pagnes, long bolts of fabric wrapped round their waists; young people in pants and T-shirts bearing the names of western products and places. A group forms around each gal, bringing the boat well up onto the beach. Those who have been fishing jump out, and the gal is deftly brought to rest on a rolling platform of spongy palm stumps.

For a few minutes there is much animated talking. People are shaking hands and greeting one another in the long, elaborate incantation of family names and familiar salutations. It is important that those who have been absent from the family life of the village be addressed individually and welcomed back. They are again at home.

Then begins the distribution of the catch. People reach into the gal, lift out the fish, make little piles in the sand. Nearby, women sit with large plastic basins filled with sea water. The women douse the fish as they begin to scale and clean them, splashing the flapping fish with salty water as they slip the scales from the flesh. A small number of dull knives lie on the sand; they are shared among the women. Occasionally, a younger girl will get to help. She rolls up her pagne, squats low on the sand, grabs a fish and begins to work.

Not far away, dogs scratch the sand, whimper and drop themselves into the cooler depressions they have excavated as they wait for scraps and bones. They are dirty brown and bony, almost feral scavengers in this culture, wary of people but unable to live without them too. The female must be in heat: as she slumps down into her temporary pit a timid male inches closer. She closes her eyes, and he begins to lick her vulva, a slim bit of gratification that he will get this day. She snarls, snaps at him, sends him off, then returns to her hungry sleep.

We have found the woman we are looking for, a friend of Vieux's. She is cradling an infant, a little girl whose hair is plaited with bright fabric bows. Without hesitation, Vieux takes the child so that the woman can get our fish. It is clear that Vieux has cared for infants. The woman explains that the catch has not been good that day and that we should simply take the several small fish that she offers—for nothing. We don't need much fish but do not want to leave without having paid for some of the labor.

Maalik sees a much bigger fish—a fine, fleshy *chof*—that we can take. "It's too big for you," she argues. We buy it at a price good for her. She turns to her friend, takes the other's knife, and cleans the chof for us. Vieux hands the baby to me so that he can get salt and charcoal from a seller in the village. He returns in a few minutes with what we need for our dinner, I hand the baby to the woman, she thanks me in French. We turn to go.

The way back is quiet and dark—there is not yet electricity along this coast though the Italians and Germans have already lobbied the government in Dakar for electric lines. The surf drowns out the sounds of Toubab Diallo, and Vieux gets the fire ready for our fish. Soon the glowing charcoal gives off its distinctive, woody smoke. I slice up onions and potatoes, and Maalik brings chairs into the cool evening breeze. Below us, Toubab Diallo gathers round its evening fires and smoking pots of fish. Dakar and the life of the city seem so far away.

Chapter Five
Exchange Program

They said that we would love the climate on the highlands in Madagascar. The best of both worlds: mangoes and coconuts grow alongside of strawberries, apples, and peaches. The few books I could find all showed the capital Antananarivo with pleasant, cobbled streets and stretches of cultivated parks. A few pages later, the inevitable photos of sandy beaches with swaying palms and the ylang-ylang in bloom, the tree with the fabulous scent. Or litchi trees, Christmas-like with their great pendent sprays of red nuts. A paradise.

The people at the State Department told me that we would love the Malagasy, who are quiet but warm. The woman on the other end of the receiver announced that she would live permanently in Madagascar if she could. I tried to imagine what this woman was like, what she looked like. Her voice had a pinched, nervous quality to it; and she kept interrupting or contradicting her colleague. It was a conference call from Washington—where I had come for a briefing—to the American Embassy in Antananarivo, and I remember thinking how far away the people on the other end of the phone line were. And they all talked with such assumed assurance about the country I knew only from books and briefings.

I also remember that I wasn't prepared for the call: I didn't have a store of questions for the embassy officials. I must not have appeared curious—even interested, at least in their terms. But after all, I had been notified of my assignment very late. "Where? Madagascar?" I remember saying on the phone when they had called a month earlier with news that I would be teaching at the university in Antananarivo. I had had no clue where the country was located. In the library's encyclopedia I had trouble finding an entry on Madagascar. It was 1988; I learned that I needed to look under the nation's new name, Malagasy Republic.

As I sat in that beige office on L'Enfant Plaza, it all seemed unreal. My wife Jill sensed the absurdity: me on a conference call listening to Americans I didn't know who were sitting in a similarly beige office 9,000 miles away while an

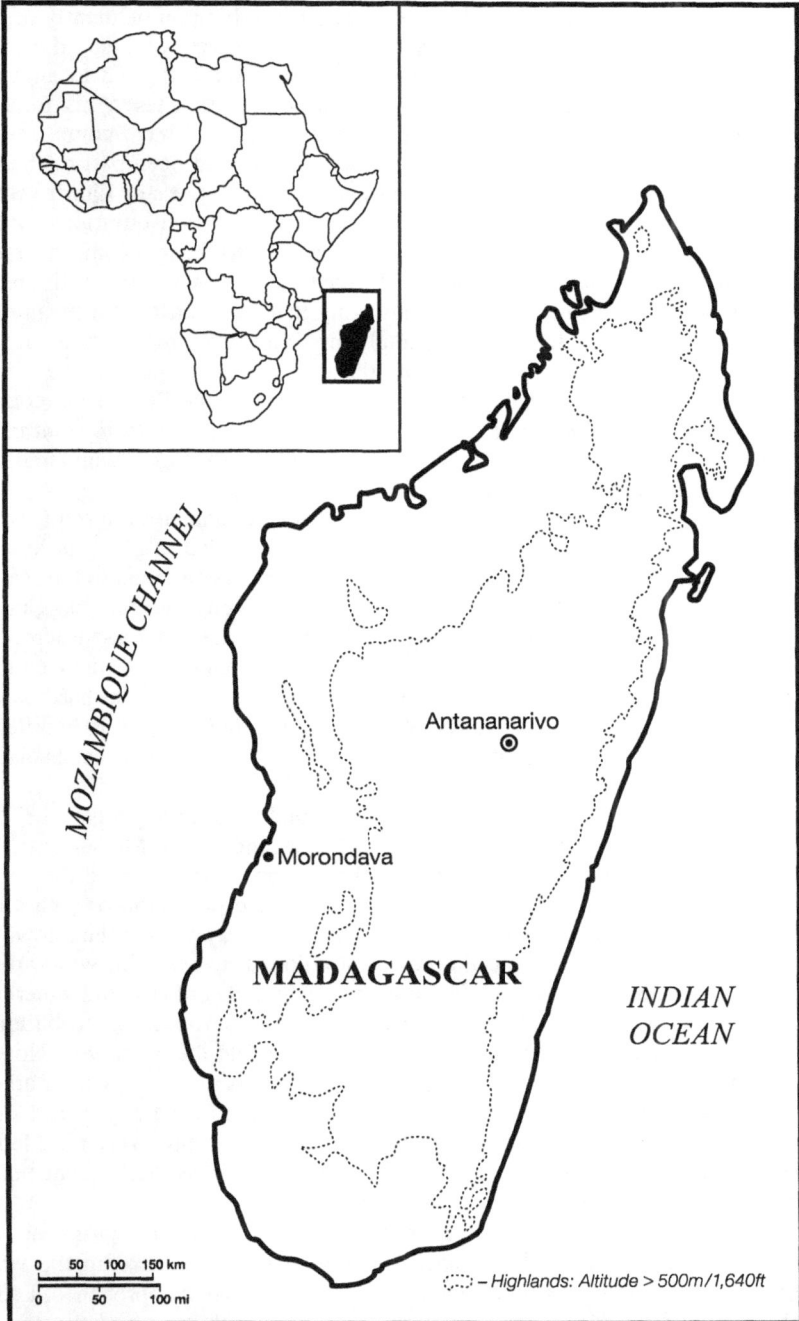

MOZAMBIQUE CHANNEL

Antananarivo
◉

● Morondava

MADAGASCAR

INDIAN OCEAN

| 0 | 50 | 100 | 150 km |
| 0 | | 50 | 100 mi |

⟨⟩ – *Highlands: Altitude > 500m / 1,640ft*

impatient bald man behind an oak veneer desk in Washington petulantly offered commands like "Ask about the money," "Find out what kind of malarial medication you need," "Tell them you have a child, and you will need to engage a nanny, at least someone to wash diapers." He was getting testy; his forehead kept wrinkling up as he produced questions that I should have come up with myself. He told me that he had done Madagascar; he had been part of the embassy staff, now returned as an expert on that country. I guess he didn't want to become permanent there. He could have answered his own questions, but he insisted that I demonstrate some sort of personal initiative by posing questions myself in this artificial way. Flustered, I asked the embassy staff on the phone what the Malagasy people were like, knowing that I couldn't get a meaningful answer to this question anyway. Amazingly, my informants went on and on for a number of minutes—expensive, long-distance minutes—about the ethnic groups, cultural and linguistic variations on the island, the Polynesian connection. As they spoke I watched the bald man pace back and forth in front of the wall-size map of Africa jabbed with lots of colored push-pins. I wondered how many of these pins the man had done.

What a surprise, then, when we landed at the Antananarivo airport, which looks out over hills long ago denuded of trees and eroded in great gashes that run red when January torrents sweep the soil to the rivers and then to the sea. No ylang-ylang, no swaying coconuts. Or the trip into the city, our taxi hugging the side of the road to let carts pass, stopping for the crossing of a zebu herd, hurtling over chuck-holes or hardened mounds of cow dung. No quaint colonial cobbles. And people everywhere—people on foot, barefoot on the hard-packed red soil, carrying blackened sacks of charcoal on their backs or bundles of rushes, prodding wizened goats, balancing enamel bowls on their heads as they clutched skinny kids to their sides.

Well, they were right about one thing: I learned to love the people.

It began with Sister Lucy. We met her the second day in Madagascar. The Political Officer from the Embassy had taken us on a drive around the capital city. I remember the steep hills covered with escaped poinsettia or naturalized bougainvillea and the narrow roads that snaked their way up and then down the ancient, quieted summits. And the decaying colonial homes with wrap-around verandahs that look out over treeless blue horizons, fields of rice and watercress in the valleys below. And lots of churches—square European stone buildings next to palms and arching jacaranda. I learned later that the country of Norway had made Madagascar a national mission project. It wasn't a mirage after all: the bevy of blue-eyed blond children that I saw in this part of the city were Nordic kids raised in highland tropics. I wondered what their dreams were like, fed on stories of fjords and snow and dewberries and herrings as well as encounters with zebu and lemurs and banana and frangipani.

The driver had to pull over for a moment to let a procession pass—or what we took to be a procession. A black Lincoln—so wide it took up the whole roadway—was making its way up to the top of the hill. As it approached, I could make out four American flags, stuck to the hood and the trunk of the car; the flags waved proudly in the tropical breeze. Passers-by stopped, moved out of the way, and looked down at the ground as the vehicle forged ahead. The extra-thick, darkened glass kept us from identifying the passenger as the American ambassador, on her to work that day. It was the daily routine, this procession to the Embassy. Of course everyone knew it was the Americans. Even the French embassy personnel drove around (or were driven around) in more modest, more practical Peugeots and Renaults. I imagined some Washington mandate that all State Department personnel "buy American"—and hence the Detroit monolith. I asked if the addition of the armored glass was a result of the general paranoia that State Department personnel live with, especially after Iran.

"You're right," our guide the Political Officer said. "We have instituted a number of safety features in case of internal trouble." I was sure that the over-sized Lincoln was not such a safety feature.

She continued, as if reading from a manual: "Our residences are provided with round-the-clock security guards, two on a shift. In addition, we have direct radio connection to the Marine post and to the ambassador." Outside our car, a couple of barefoot Malagasy walked by, their backs bowed under the weight of bags of charcoal they lugged. They looked at the uneven ground as they headed down the hill. Behind them a woman with an infant strapped to her back; she carried a rush satchel filled with flowers—fantastic proteas, big and vivid red. Just then it was hard for me to imagine the threat that the Malagasy posed.

The car pulled up in front of a large wooden gate. The buzzer didn't work, so the driver had to pound on the rose-colored wood—the entrance to the home of Sister Lucy's order. "You'll want to meet Sister Lucy," the Political Office said. She assumed knowledge of people's feelings about everything. At the time I was wondering why a religious order dedicated to life among the poor would live behind high walls and locked gates. A moment later, a young Malagasy woman pushed open the gate.

"*Manao ahaona,*" we all said. We had practiced our greetings, however much we mangled the pronunciation.

The young woman smiled as she quietly answered something we couldn't understand. Our language development had gotten no further than basic greetings.

Sister Lucy walked over to greet us. She was just like the description—thin and small, with short black hair. Her eyes were brown and deep and appeared to smile as she spoke. She extended a bony hand with long fingers and spoke to us in good English: "I am so happy to meet you. Welcome to Madagascar."

This was a woman who had given her entire adult life to living among people that weren't her own, though we didn't know where Sister Lucy came from. Our guide thought that she was Indian, and we knew that she had spent some years in South Africa. Certainly that country could have been the lesson in gross social inequity that inspired in her a lifelong ambition to redress human wrong. In any case, it didn't take long to learn that this was a person who clearly felt that her life had purpose, real human purpose, and who worked hard—for others and for herself. Even among the intolerant embassy community, her name had a kind of halo effect: what this woman did was good, even though the work did little to increase the GNP or further structural adjustment policies.

"Maybe you'd like to buy some of our embroidery," she offered, ushering us into the small combination sitting room-general store. Sister Lucy had organized the local women into cooperatives in an effort to get them a small share in the money economy. The women stitched fantastic scenes onto white napkins— for us to wipe our hands on at home. Another group of women wove table cloths, which would protect the wood on our tables. Still another group fashioned Christmas ornaments with appliqué—to hang from pines and spruces unknown in this place. But the money they made was theirs.

Sister Lucy was very skillful at cajoling us—now her clientele—to buy, and buy a lot. "Don't forget all your family members," she added. "I can have more of these napkins made for you if you need 12 or 18." She uncovered new patterns as we pawed through the piles of cotton and linen. We all bought heartily—who could refuse a saint?

There was another visitor to the convent-shop that day, an expatriate American woman married to a road engineer from Switzerland. While Sister Lucy listened, Prue went through an oral résumé of herself with a conciseness that comes from years of offering such information to people whom you would probably not see again. We learned that Prue had given up nursing in order to follow François to this job in exotic Madagascar. With self-deprecating humor, she described herself as a woman with "no kids and a husband who is always off draining swamps or carving roadways through rocks and trees." Meanwhile, Prue stayed back in their big, empty, hilltop home equidistant from Europe and California. She added, finally, that François had promised that this would be his last foreign assignment and that they could return to California as soon as the road was complete.

As things turned out, we became good friends with Prue. Oddly enough, it was the napkin episode that brought us together.

And, yielding to Sister Lucy's suggestion, Prue did want more: another set of napkins with intricate natural scenes from Madagascar—lemurs, ravinala trees, bamboo—stitched in brilliant colors. "I can take you to meet the woman who does this work," Sister Lucy said. "You can tell her what more you want. It will be good for you to meet her."

Looking back on this now, I wonder if Sister Lucy knew just what she was really saying. I feel quite sure that she did.

A couple of weeks later, I accompanied Prue and Sister Lucy to meet the embroiderer. I was curious to meet real Malagasy people, who, I was sure, would be different from the relatively wealthy and educated class of Malagasy that I got to know through my work or through the disenchanted diplomatic community that felt stranded on this distant island.

With Sister Lucy, Prue and I climbed up the steep hillsides of the city following stone steps that had in places collapsed long ago or that were overgrown with lianas. Occasionally we had to side-step streams of sewage in its trickle down the mountain side. Bits of waste paper and plastic clung like perverse blossoms to shrubs. The thin atmosphere made the effort difficult even though the temperature was typically pleasant.

The villas with open verandahs gave way to more modest wooden homes as we moved away from the main road. Behind the wooden structures we could make out smaller places still—home-made mud brick hovels with roofs stitched together of tin pieces, wooden planks, and cardboard. Sister Lucy deftly made her way through the muddy yard to the open door of one of the shacks. She knew where she was taking us. She went up to a woman who had been standing just inside the shack.

I heard her *Manao ahaona* though I didn't even take a stab at the greeting this time. Prue and I had to bow low in order to get through the doorway. We nodded meaninglessly to the woman, so gaunt and so broken that she could barely grasp the hands we extended by way of greeting. She never raised her eyes—not even to Sister Lucy—and spoke only in answer to Sister Lucy's gentle questions. There was one room, not much bigger than our bathroom back in the States. The room was lighted by no windows, save for the doorway, which served the dual function of entry and light source. Little red puddles had formed on the mud floor; in the corner, away from us and the mud, a group of children huddled together.

There were children—four of them, all very young. They too were quiet. Out of the folds of her habit Sister Lucy produced small dry biscuits that she took over to give to them. Listlessly, they reached for the food, maybe their only meal that day, certainly that morning. The one in the corner—a little girl with braided reddened hair—caught Prue's attention. I looked at the child for a few seconds then self-consciously turned my eyes to the other corner with its small mound of blankets and clothes. The little girl must have been about two.

It was an uncomfortable meeting. Yet Sister Lucy insisted upon our showing the woman what embroidery Prue wanted done; it seemed as if she held us in that little house. She made quiet asides to Prue in English: "Tell her just what colors you would like. Make sure you give her the pictures. Don't forget the sizes." Prue produced pictures, measurements. She was happy to give the woman the advance for the purchase of the materials—a big advance, much more than the total cost of the embroidery—pulling a number of large, multi-color bills from her wallet and handing them to Sister Lucy, our cultural interpreter. The whole pile amounted to only a few dollars.

I felt awkward, standing there in that dismal hut, thinking of all the reasons my life was so different from what I saw around me, an alien world. I wondered what sort of adult this kind of childhood experience would breed. Would the children—if they lived—remain listless and hopeless as they aged? Would they continue—in their adult lives—to make small demands of the people and the world around them? Meanwhile, Prue kept looking at the sullen children, who barely moved. After some anxious minutes and a nod from Sister Lucy, we thanked our host and said goodbye, *Veloma.*

On the way down the hill, Sister Lucy was quite talkative. "You know she has no husband, Nirina Rasolofo. No income—and all those children." It was then that we learned that the little girl was also named Nirina, *Beloved.* "I get what business I can for Nirina Rasolofo, though it is not enough. She is often sick. We don't have a doctor any more in our community here. There is only so much we are able to do for her." Sister Lucy spoke frankly, as if to another member of her order whose life was spent trying to improve others' chances.

Though I did not know Prue well, I could imagine what she was thinking. *We could take the child. He does not need me enough; his world is almost complete without me. She will need me. I will create a world for her, a safe world. She could become ours, one of us.*

I had heard these thoughts before, in the quiet of my own life. Jill and I had been married for six years and could not conceive. We wanted to have children; neither of us felt quite complete without kids. First there was the embarrassment—waiting month after month, year after year, while friends' children were born, grew out of diapers and into school. Then the tests, the bedside basal temperature charts, the plotting of pregnancy potential against mucous consistency. There was plenty of guilt—the silent blaming of each other, our combined inadequacy. For some reason, it was easy for me to assume that we would some-day adopt. But I hadn't counted on Jill's tacit but powerful resistance to that thought.

So it was ironic that she should become pregnant just about the time we learned that we might be leaving the US to hole up in tropical Africa for a while. Whether through the sudden procreative intervention of some deity or through fortuitous biochemical processes, we greeted the birth of our first child just before leaving the States for Madagascar. We had our own family.

But for Prue and François—there was no question that they would adopt. Prue saw to that.

The following day she returned to the convent with a response to Sister Lucy's veiled question. "I thought you would make a suitable parent," Sister Lucy said coyly. "I am sure that Nirina Rasolofo will agree. I will talk to her first and let you know." Not many days later, a message came from the embassy secretary: "Sister Lucy says that all will be okay."

Surprisingly, the embassy staff were quite helpful in organizing the adoption. It was as if they had been through all this many times. The Political Officer generously offered to intercede for Prue at government agencies in town, where you had to know whom to bribe in order to get to the decision-makers, who, it turned out, always got the biggest bribe of all. She found baby clothes for Prue, even a used playpen and some imported toys. What an unexpected application of her political savvy. And all the while she kept commenting on this "act of generosity" of Prue's, as if she had given the child a new life.

I couldn't help wondering what Nirina might recall of her Malagasy self once she was removed to suburban America or secure Switzerland. I wondered how her life in that hut could possibly prepare her for her future in a place so distant and different. I wondered if she, one day, would resent being ripped from familiar—though scarcely succoring—spaces. I wondered what dreams that child would bring with her to the country that, like its ambassadors, had to consider itself bigger and better than all others. I wondered if she would dream of hunger in a nation that casually wastes food or stuffs itself on fatty, poorly-prepared fast food. I worried that she would dream of blue hills and red mangoes in the grey patchwork of our regular sidewalks and concrete strip malls. I didn't try to explain my worries to the Political Officer. I didn't voice them to Prue either.

The formalities took about a month and a half. Once every several days Prue would head up the hill armed with food and provisions for the Rasolofo family and the special child. Occasionally, I would accompany her. Nirina Rasolofo accepted the gifts though she said very little. We looked for obvious signs of concern—or fear—for her child. Nothing we could read. On the last visit, she picked up little Nirina, gave her the slightest of hugs, and handed the child to Prue. We turned to go. "*Attendez*," she interrupted in French as she reached in to a pile of cloth into the corner. In an odd sort of emotive flurry, she produced the embroidered napkins, wrapped in newsprint.

A few days later, Jill and I made our way up the snaking cobbled streets to the stretch of tall orange-brick houses that sit facing the cliffs that fall from the front of the Queen's Palace, an important tourist-stop in present-day Antananarivo. In the nineteenth century, the Malagasy queen—in a fit of xenophobic anxiety—had foreign missionaries thrown off these rocky heights. Now, gently curving avenues lined with jacarandas—planted by the French—and the grassy city soccer field stand where those early ambassadors fell. With the palace behind us, we knocked on the rosewood door. We had come to pay our respects to the new family.

Nirina had made the trip well: she accepted the food and the solicitation given to her. Over time her weight would pick up and the redness in her hair would fade. Her second mother was tired and very happy.

Jill handed over the baby gifts we had brought with us—a bib, a plastic rattle, a mobile with shapes suspended from it. While Prue opened the packages, I noticed the stack of new napkins underneath a pile of baby things. They had not been opened.

I folded back the newsprint. Everything was there, finely done on the white linen: the lemurs with their ring-tails; bright green spikes of the ravinala, the plant they call the Travellers' Tree; red-brick buildings with tile roofs and nodding palm trees—beautiful and familiar features of this place so unlike the world we knew as home. There was an extra one, at the bottom of the pile—the figure of a white woman cradling a brown child and the word *Veloma* stitched in bright blue irregular letters at the bottom.

I could not decide if it was a token of the exchange or a sign of loss. I guess it was both.

Chapter Six
Missionary

The Rift Valley slices through eastern Africa, where the clash of massive geologic forces can be seen in the great plateaus that rise sharply and unhesitatingly from the sandy landmass and in the constellation of deep lakes strung like stars along ancient and mute fault lines. In eastern Africa these cool highlands became home to Europeans—explorers, missionaries, settlers—who came in waves after the region was platted and defined by David Livingstone, the intrepid Scot, whose meeting with the American newspaperman Stanley in 1871, at Ujiji, on the shores of Lake Tanganyika, thrilled a reading public on two continents, manifestly certain at the time that the destiny of Africa included European players.

Stanley could not persuade Livingstone to leave Africa, despite the explorer's poor health. With his small band of African helpers, Livingstone forged ahead in his quest to find and map the source of the life-giving Nile, issuing, as he felt it had to, from one of these opaline lakes. Livingstone had long before sent his young and struggling family back to Scotland—to wonder at a father who preferred Africa to home and who was energized by uncharted tropical landscapes, not the climate of family and cultural affinity. As he wished, Livingstone died at work—in 1873—totally engaged in his greatest quest, distant from the sound of cities, from the day-to-day demands of family responsibility, from the stultifying obligations of clerical life in Christian Europe.

The renegade clergyman spent his last days in the village of Chitambo, part of Zambia on today's maps. One day towards the end of the season of rains, Livingstone's friends entered his hut near the sprawling palaver tree. The hut was uncharacteristically quiet though typically tidy. Notebooks lay open with recent work—sketches, lists of plants, catalogs of names. Makeshift shelves sat carefully stacked with papers and books. Then they came upon his body rigid in a posture of prayer, kneeling lifeless alongside the bed. Knowing where Livingstone's affections truly lay, they lifted up and smoothed out the body, then re-

moved the heart and ceremoniously buried it outside, where it could meld forever with the dark, red forces of the African earth.

The missionary's eldest son had died almost a decade earlier, after he had
turned his back on Europe and the beatified ghosts of this father only to perish
gratuitously in a prisoner-of-war camp in the United States. In a drama oddly
akin to his father's mission in Africa, he fought alongside northern forces in the
Civil War to liberate unwillingly expatriate Africans in the New World. The
boy, Robert, had just newly enlisted when he was taken prisoner and sent to a
prison camp in Salisbury, North Carolina.

Ironically, Robert had fled to the United States to escape emotional con-
finement in England. First he ran away from boarding school, then he unsuc-
cessfully tried to chase down his father, who was at that moment in 1863
camped somewhere along the Zambezi River. Robert had a mission of his own:
he went to Africa to give his father the explorer news of his wife's death. But
there was no meeting with the man who had abandoned his five children and a
wife who later drank herself to death. Despite the abandonment (or, more probably, because of it) the boy did not feel he could live up to his father's international reputation as a moral trail-blazer. In a letter that reached the missionary
father after Robert's death, the lost son admitted that, in America, he had
changed his name to avoid dishonor to his father.

His father's name was not without tarnish, however. With the exception of
the mercenary Welsh-American Stanley, Livingstone managed to disaffect almost all Europeans he came in contact with, always preferring the company of
Africans. Most of his adult life he spent wending his way through savannahs
thick with tall grasses and spare and spiny broadleaf evergreens or paddling
down rivers swallowed up in the interior of the continent. In his last days, did
Livingstone yet consider himself a member of a "superior race", as he had written in his diary on an earlier trip? And did he manage to "elevate the African
members of the human family," as he had, earlier, wished? Or had he begun to
lament the presence of Europeans in his pristine Africa? Did the unofficial colonial policy of "opening the great heart of Africa" up to commerce and trade begin to appall the missionary-explorer? And, how could a man raised in the bald-
ing highlands of Scotland willfully and completely sever his ties with his native
land and people in order to find shifting but sustaining citizenship among African ethnic groups he had only recently come to know?

No one will know what the missionary-explorer might have answered. But
his African friends knew the depth of their love: they labored for nine months to
carry the heartless and disintegrating body overland to the sea, where it made the
final sea-journey back to England and a state burial in Westminster Abbey in
1883 while its soul ranges among blue hills and the high lakes of the Rift Valley
even today.

***

Even a quick trip to southern Africa ought to be enough to convince you
that Livingstone's ghost still inhabits these high, deep lakes and rolling lowlands
of the Rift Valley. There is a Livingstone town in Zambia, just across from Vic-

toria Falls. On the Zimbabwe side of the falls, a stone statue of the explorer commands an impressive view of the cataracts and looks out over the fringe of rainy forest that grips the edges of those steep cliffs in this otherwise gray and sandy landscape. It was Livingstone who gave these magnificent falls their enduring imperial name, one that does not recall their more poetic and appropriate Shona description, "the-cloud-that-thunders," but which instead honors a queen whose nation was engaged in mission work of its own—colonialism.

Maybe Livingstone could have been persuaded to broadcast the Shona name had he been able to approach the falls from the air. In the midst of a vast brown plain dotted with irregular patches of spare and spiny trees an enormous cloud arises thick and wet, not from an open umbilicus in the sky but from the snaking river below. The falls and the river are outlined in bright green, like the bold edges map-makers draw to distinguish nation from nation. And the quiet of the savannah is broken by a sound—distant and muffled at first—that crescendos into a constant liquid roar as you approach those unlikely wet cliffs. But when he arrived, Livingstone had only a canoe to bring him down river, and he had a legacy to bequeath to his adopted continent.

Not far from the falls, in the damp north of the small country of Malawi, the town of Livingstonia sits at the foot of the cool and lush Nkhotakota plateau where zebras and wildebeest graze on the tall grass. It would be harder to imagine a place more distant—physically and culturally—from Scotland. As the lake follows fault lines to the south, forests of teak and mahogany thin out. The lake withdraws into swampy lowlands full of malaria that become the source of the Shire, the muddy river that makes its way south, bathing populations of water buffalo, elephants, and humans along its way. The civil war in Mozambique in the 80s and 90s chased thousands of refugees to this relatively safe but sorry place. New huts huddle together in make-shift villages too new to have a name, the thatch in tufts on the roofs barely sufficient to keep out the rain. Small corrals of thorny twigs and parched palm branches pen in skinny goats. Even more people crowded onto tired land. This is unpleasant country, hotter than the highlands and drier and less productive. The Shire eventually joins up with the fabled Zambezi, a river Livingstone charted for the Royal Geographical society in England. And before the union of the rivers, the forest breaks up completely as it gives way to some stony outcrop or another—trailing geologic involvements of the Rift. Then the sunny African city that bears the name of its impossible homologue in Scotland, Blantyre.

A large Scots Presbyterian church welcomes visitors to the city. Its twin brick spires stretch into the sky, which might recall Scotland if the air were not so perfumed by pungent plumerias nearby. Inside, the dark tropical wood of the cross-beams might be mistaken for stained ash or oak. The hymnal includes Old 100, as would be expected, though there is a parallel text in Chewa. Livingstone can still be found here.

***

About 300 miles to the east, across the Mozambique Channel, the Malagasy town of Morondava sits at the end of a stretch of paved road that links this hot outpost with the interior highlands of Madagascar. The road is a gift of the Chinese, who built the road—with cute little red pagodas that serve as rest-stops—in hopes of preferment from the left-leaning Malagasy government of the 70s and 80s. The unnatural pavement is generally free of traffic in this sparsely-populated, semi-arid part of the Giant Red Island—not much commercial reason to drive to Morondava, the largest town for many miles.

Much of the Malagasy population lives on the temperate highlands, where the climate is never extreme. That land was long ago denuded of trees; the grassy ridges now appear strangely blue in the distance, and the soil, gouged and eroded by monsoon rains, shines blood-red where the latest chasm has opened in the supine body of the island. In their zeal to create grazing land for their hump-backed zebu cattle, the Malagasy destroyed the ancient highland forests on their island; the epidermal grasses that took the place of ebony and teak trees scarcely hold back the rain or keep moisture close to the soil surface. And so the island bleeds into the sea, which gives sad testimony to the origin of its popular name.

The temperature rises dramatically as you come down from the cool highlands. The path down the escarpment pours you out onto the flat coastal plain, and the humidity increases with every drop in elevation. For a while, the road runs in the direction of the next stop to the south, the South Pole. Then the road turns east and takes you through spare forests of royal palms and, later, great groves of bottle-shaped baobabs on the last stretch to the coast. It was not so much the town of Morondava but the Catholic Mission that I had come to see.

The Mission was well-known throughout the country. Even the savagely secular State Department people spoke fondly of it—or at least of Father Joe, the American priest. I had heard about the school that the Mission ran; later I wrote and asked if I could visit. A prompt reply welcomed me and explained that Father Joe would be my host.

Morondava circles round the Mission, a collection of cinder-block structures that includes a church, an elementary school, a school for the deaf, a large meeting hall, a clinic, and an assortment of smaller buildings. Most of the Malagasy live outside this development in little huts fashioned of bamboo poles and palm fronds. The homes of the few Europeans are square block, with louvered doors and windows, painted in pastel colors. From time to time, cyclones crash down the Mozambique Channel, smashing homes and lives in heavy rains and strong winds. The last cyclone had blown ashore not long before my visit to Morondava. It had not been terribly destructive—only a few palms and an outbuilding had been lost in the Mission, and an unknown number of zebu, chickens, and dogs had been carried off towards Antarctica.

For most Americans in Madagascar, the Mission and Father Joe were synonymous. From the first, I really liked Father Joe. As I peeled myself from the sticky seat of the car he grabbed my hand and shook it vigorously as he said hello. His thinning hair was swept to the side of this large head, and his paunchy stomach bulged underneath his plain cassock, belying any hint of asceticism.

There was something irreverent about his casual manner and his careless appearance that appealed to me. Fearing holy formality, I was pleasantly surprised by his open friendliness and by his thick Boston accent that had not tempered despite his 12 years' internment here on the other side of the world in the company of French and Polish monastics and Malagasy-speaking parishioners.

"You will have a tour of the school in the morning," one of the priests said in French. "For now, *reposez-vous*." But Father Joe got hold of me instead; he led me inside the main Mission building.

On the balcony of the second floor we found chairs where we could sit and talk without interruption. A young man—a novice perhaps—brought tepid soft drinks and glasses, set them on a table, bowed and left. Flies buzzed around our heads, and mosquitoes hovered just outside the revealing glare of sunlight. Despite the drowsy hour of the hot afternoon, it didn't take much to get Joe talking about his life in Madagascar. He told me about one of his congregations 40 kilometers from Morondava. There was of course no public transport to the village, so he walked there and back on foot.

"You have to start early in the day," he began, "and take plenty of water—not to mention medication for the shits. And you have to know where to stop for food and rest. What little I know of this place, the Malagasy have taught me. They know this land. They know where the sand hides juicy roots that you can tap and drink in the heat. And they help me along the way. Wherever I go, people offer me food and a place to sit away from the sun. I never need to ask. These are kind, generous people, and they are dignified in spite of the lousy conditions of their lives."

"What do you do for those people in the bush—I mean, what do you say to them?"

"I have no good answer for you," Father Joe said, smiling. "But I can tell you one thing. See that hut over there, next to the swamp?" He pointed just outside the Mission compound. "That little hut—it couldn't be more than 8-foot square—is home for a family of nine."

He paused to wave the flies from around his face.

"No windows, see? And no netting to keep out the clouds of mosquitoes at night."

I grimaced, imagining the nightly chorus of malaria-bearing hummers.

"You know what the family does? They take turns, they sleep in shifts. One half of the family crouches at one end of the hut while the others get four or five hours of sleep. Then, somewhere in the middle of the night, they all shift places. Amazing, isn't it?"

I asked the expected dumb question. "Why don't they get a bigger place?"

"Because they don't see that it's necessary. They don't think about their comfort at all." The priest stopped to wipe his sweaty face. "They don't think it's necessary," he repeated. "Their own physical comfort is not of great importance to them. They give real meaning to the word *selfless*."

He paused, as if to let his words sink in, then continued. "So, what have I to offer them? Not much—some time, a chance for an education if they want to send a relative to the Mission school. Maybe some anti-malarials for a sick child or grandparent—that's *if* I've gotten to the medicine-box before going out. A prayer for more rain, or less rain, or an end to structural adjustment policies that impose taxes and never bring cheaper rice or fish. Mostly just my dumpy American presence in their Malagasy village. It means a lot to them to be able to host and take care of a stranger."

Father Joe stopped talking. We sat quietly for a few moments; the intense heat was almost palpable. His brown eyes were sunk deep into his round face; his skin was creased on his forehead and near his eyes. From the way he moved and the wear on his face, I figured that he must have been 45 or 50 years old though there was a child-like quality about him. He got up abruptly and announced that we should see the chapel, showing me the way out the back of the Mission.

The sun was beginning to set somewhere over Mozambique and Malawi to the west; orange rays scudded across the Channel and set the town on fire. We crossed the compound yard and moved towards a small structure off behind the school. Except for the corrugated zinc roof that supported a yellow bougainvillea, all thick and grasping and green, the little white-washed chapel was open. No doors or windows to close up and shut out. Inside, a few rough wooden benches and an altar made from a single polished tree stump over whose ringed surface a brightly-colored fabric hung down towards the packed-earth floor. Nothing on top of the altar, no chalice for blood or monstrance for the host. Behind and above the stump, a small breach in the wall let in the sun's light. Though I did not consider myself a religious person, I recognized that this was a holy place. And I knew that I was in the company of a modest, holy man. I had accomplished the most important part of my visit.

***

The return flight to the west from Madagascar heads over Mozambique and over the place that Livingstone explored, now called Malawi. From the plane you may be able to make out the blue haze of highlands that extend on two sides of a broad brownish valley, the Rift Valley. Eventually the plane may cross Lake Albert and Lake Victoria whose strange names show why, for years, history and geography were considered a single school subject: those that name the world also write its history. After the plane swoops past Albert, the tablelands of the African continent break away and the low humid-green Congo basin spreads out below. This is the "heart of darkness" that writers who came after Livingstone named and mythologized for western readers forever.

David Livingstone was one of those westerners who called the "heart of darkness" home. The adoption of the new continent may, for him, have been easier had he not left a wife and children in Scotland. Or, like the Indian husband who in good conscience renounces his family in order to become a fakir, was Livingstone successful in absolving himself of responsibilities for his former life?

If so, then his attitude towards his adopted African family was surely paternalistic. In *Missionary Travels*, the collection of Livingstone's letters and journal entries, the clergyman announced that he had come to Africa as a "servant of a government that desires to elevate the more degraded portions of the human family." On one hand, it must have been difficult for the religious man to spend his entire adult life in the company of inferiors. On the other, his living among Africans must to him have been constant proof of his generosity: the gift of the "superior servant." And the legacy of his imperialist agenda can still be seen throughout southern Africa.

Yet, I believe that Father Joe found a middle path—a way to retain his own culture and beliefs while accepting other ways of being. For him, Africa was not a religious frontier, not a place to test alien ideas of individuality or of the immutable distance between human and spirit worlds. For him, the missionary vocation was a life-long commitment to considering how to conduct one's life in the company of others. I think that when Father Joe's time comes and he is laid in the sandy earth in the Morondava Mission cemetery, his spirit will be at peace. There should be no monument to draw attention to his living or to his passing, only perhaps a majestic weedy palm or a vigorous indigenous vine.

Chapter Seven
Native Speaker

How curious—a high tea, with cream and scones, served from a carved oak table on the spacious veranda of Cecil Rhodes' former residence way up in the Nyanga mountains of Zimbabwe. And how wonderful—I was starving after the six hours-ride in the Mercedes bus, and it was still well before the dinner hour. We ate greedily and drank in the view—down through forests of pines and eucalypts to a lake surrounded by bamboo stands and tufts of brilliant crimson anthurium. It was overcast and cool, and water dripped from broad leaves onto bright green grass and beds of tender, elsewhere annual, flowers—pretty single petunias, tall larkspur, golden pot marigolds. It didn't take much imagination to see sycamore for the gum trees and substitute cattails for the bamboo, this was so much like the country Rhodes had willingly left behind not even a hundred years before. And when we heard her talking, in her affected British accent, we weren't sure where we were.

"This is the region my husband, the Prime Minister, most deeply loves," she announced Her *r*'s all rolled, and final consonants got lots of extra time, each word exploding with its concluding consonant. *Husb-a-n-d,* said slowly, with deliberation, the *n* swallowed as the *d* came forward in her mouth. Her eyes lowered as she lingered over the words *Prime Minister*; I expected her to curtsey or to bow.

I was distracted by a splash on the lake, then returned to my eavesdropping: "—like to come up here when we can get away from state affairs. You know—official dinners, delegations, E.T.C., E.T.C."

That's just how she did it—spelling out the initial letters of *etcetera,* and with a flourish of her arm she glided down the steps to the lawn. Her retinue followed—the hotel owner, some of the staff, and a few of my group. She allowed little time for questions or comments—the monologic approach to the social art of conversation.

I can still see her clearly there against the fresh green. Her hair was tangled and held back in a pile by a colorful floral scarf. Then the enormous eyeglasses and the very round mouth. Fuchsia lipstick exceeded the confines of those small lips, creating a sensuous—if false—smile. She wasn't tall and, judging by her weight, had apparently not suffered from the local cuisine for all these years. Her clothing was an interesting accommodation to traditional wear: she wore a tailored blouse that must have come from the States and, in lieu of a skirt, a bolt of African fabric wrapped around her and secured in the front with a knot. She kept adjusting the make-shift skirt as she talked, tying and untying the knot, pulling down or yanking up on the cloth, which reached all the way to the ground. From time to time the yanking on the skirt revealed her tiny feet, squeezed into red cloth slippers browned from their contact with the soil. I wondered how those minute, almost unprotected feet could support all that weight and motion.

Happily, she permitted us to call her Marian—instead of Madame Prime Minister. I was sure that she would insist on formality, but I was wrong. As it turned out, we spent the better part of several days with Marian Mutare. We were all given explicit lessons on the correct pronunciation of her married name. She insisted on taking our study group through the region when she learned that we were all from the States, some of us former Buckeyes like herself. So we got to know the lovely highlands of Zimbabwe with a near-native guide, one who, like us, had grown up in another weather and world.

I was fascinated by her. Over the course of the next few days bits and pieces of her past slipped out as she spoke. To this was added information that my travelling companions—university professors used to garnering information from unusual places—came up with. We put her story together.

She had grown up in a conservative, self-proclaimed Christian family. After high school at a private Christian academy in her small, southwestern Ohio city, she managed to get to Ohio State and not to one of those little Christian colleges socially transfixed sometime in the 1950s. Did she even know why she insisted on the 60,000-student school stuck in the middle of Columbus, the city that marketers have picked to try out commercial products because it has such a remarkably average population? Was it the everyday secular world that she was, unwittingly, looking for? And why did the rigid parents finally relent? Was it because she had been a model adolescent—obedient, diligent—but typically subversive? She couldn't have known it was at OSU that the future Prime Minister was studying, a student from a third-world nation with a full scholarship from a missionary society. He was living testimony to the benefits of entente between religious and secular worlds.

Maybe the two met at a Bible study or maybe at a Wednesday-night church service. One thing was for sure: her upbringing had taught her to be certain of things and to put faith in her certainty. And after the first meeting, Marian was certain that she loved this man. His curious but correct English with its funny expressions and his dramatic gestures. The broad shoulders that left his plain shirt shuddering around his narrow waist; the deep chocolate color of his skin, his eyes deeper still, large and bright. There had been no one else before—no muscular farm boy from the next town, no square and self-denying church friend. She had never let herself dream of loving a man, much less an African one.

And then she must have brought him home. It may have been a big family event—Thanksgiving or Christmas, though she probably was more prudent and tried to ease him into the family's good graces on a nondescript Ohio winter weekend. A "guess-who's-coming-to-dinner" sequence.

What followed, however, is a matter of fact, not conjecture. Marian was not permitted to see George again, much less to date him. The dinner had been pleasant enough, though quiet and, to an insider, strained. George excused himself early, and Marian was kept back for the whispered inquisition.

In our glib academic imaginations we came up with the probable rationalizations the parents provided. At first they would have tried something like: "He's not one of us. He could never be. He's not like you. His heritage and family traditions are so different. You could never get along." Then later, after the failure of the first line of persuasion: "Things would be very difficult for him if he stayed here anyway. And you couldn't possibly go over there. Think of the filth and the bugs. What would you eat? How would you live? You couldn't even *speak* to those people."

Sometimes parents say what they shouldn't and in so doing offer challenges that their children may adopt as personal crusades. Marian left home the following day, took George with her back to campus, wrote a lengthy letter with copious quotes from the Bible, vowed to marry George and return with him to Rhodesia when his program ended, and stated that she would not return to her home until her parents recognized and accepted her choice in marriage. She sent the letter the next day and waited for a response that never came.

Then, after graduation a few months later, George Mutare and Marian Losacker, attended by a few friends from the Bible study group, were married by the university chaplain. There was no telex from Rhodesia; neither was there any acknowledgement from small-city southwestern Ohio. And Marian left Ohio later that summer, having never left the States—not even her own state of Ohio—before, her only knowledge of the world of which she was to a permanent resident a matter of the few descriptive details her husband and the limited library collection of books about Rhodesia could provide. This country never had figured in her dreams, not even in daydreams: once there, she saw herself healing leprous and consumptive children and saving the souls of wayward men with alcohol or drug problems.

Arriving in the white highlands of Rhodesia a few years before the start of the civil war in the late 70s, Marian Mutare set out immediately to learn Shona. It helped that, for a time, she and George—who had been named a regional administrator—lived in his family village in Nyanga, instead of in English-speaking Salisbury. So, those familiar objects from her American past—bobby pins, high school yearbooks, popsicle stick art projects dangling from string, piles of *Weekly Readers*—became relics of some mute, lost civilization while her mind struggled to reshape the world in the way that Shona speakers see it. She learned that, for the Shona, there is no difference between the verbs *to like* and *to want*. For the Shona therefore what you have is what you like; and in the village where everyone has pretty much what everyone else has, that is not a problem. But to say to someone that you like her blouse, you are asking for the blouse. And for the villagers, Marian personified material abundance: she was white and American. She interpreted as compliments all the remarks she used to get: "I like your dress," "I like your house," "I like your hair." That is, until she could think with a Shona mind. Then, she began to dress more simply, conceal the material fruits of her husband's position, avoid the obvious displays of her difference. When our group met her, Marian's Shona was, we were told, absolutely fluent, full of proverbs and local idioms. Nyanga Shona, the language of her husband's people, of her adopted people. The anthropologist in our group— a small man with a prickly aversion to casual conversation—labeled her ability "near-native." Her parents could never have imagined this.

But like the others I soon tired of the affected British speech and the imperial poses and gestures. In less charitable moments I wondered how easily the transition was made from Buckeye to Madame Prime Minister, a person whose social strength derived from two external sources—proximity to power and skin color. I wondered how the local Shona dealt with this outsider who swept in from somewhere beyond imagination, mastered all available idioms, and embarked on a program to improve their world. And I wondered if we all force ourselves upon the world around us, making a meaningful place for ourselves by mastering the external forms of existence.

***

It was the final day of our tour to the Nyanga region. Marian Mutare insisted that we visit a refugee camp down on the border with Mozambique. "Not far, not far," she promised, pointing her fat hand out the front window to the east. Plumes of diesel smoke stretched out behind us.

The weather changed as we drove in the Mercedes bus to the border. The cool highlands gave way to sticky, hot valleys. The skimpy rainfall, enough to keep cool highlands moist and green, was not enough to support more than an occasional blossom of faded color on the hillsides here. The road, which had been paved in Nyanga, petered out as we approached the border of the country that had been at war with itself for ten years. Ten years when nothing worked— none of the economic and political consistencies that we count on so that we can cultivate our selves and all our liberties. Ten years when an already fragile economy had collapsed completely and general anarchy kept even the informal village economy clandestine and crippled.

We jounced and jolted our way to the camp, glad for the first time on our trip that we had had our malaria prophylaxis and gamma globulin shots, trying to forget the big breakfast of eggs, tomatoes, and sausages that we had shoveled in at the hotel just a few hours earlier. We got closer to the camp, and our progress was measured by increasing numbers of children huddled in groups alongside the road. Gathered in groups of three or four, they stared blankly. Staring, barefoot, and dressed in rags. I saw my daughters in one of those faces—serious, clear-eyed, attentive—and worried about those two *other* children, four and six years old and growing up in a world antithetical to this. The bus was not surrounded by groping, outstretched hands, as some of us—in our fearful minds—imagined it would be. Rather, everyone seemed inert. It was strangely silent.

Except for Marian Mutare. As the bus lurched to a stop she jumped out, barking commands to several men standing nearby. The paltry gifts we had brought with us were unloaded—she saw to that—and the money we had collected, 65 dollars US, was handed over to an official-looking man. He thanked her and us in profuse Shona. Then, Marian Mutare started the tour of the camp she had helped to organize herself. A large group of refugees formed around Marian and the members of my own group, yet there was little noise; Marian's voice could easily be heard. She walked slowly, pointing out the milk distribution shack, the heavily-guarded storage shacks, the septic medical shack. Flies buzzed and the humidity weighed heavily on us. But the work was remarkable: Marian had found the money to create this place. Her own parents had sent money for this project, she said. Things had come a long way, I said to myself.

I left the group to find my daughters among the bystanders. The driver, a young Zimbabwean whose English I could easily understand, came with me.

"Do you know Madame Prime Minister very well, Peter?" I ventured, using the most formal English possible.

"She is well known—everyone knows her. The people they love her." I was a little surprised. "I imagine that she has had some problems adjusting to life in Zimbabwe." I was prying. "The civil war must have been hard. And for a white woman to be with an African." I knew the history enough to know of the transition from white to black rule.

"Life has not been easy for anyone." A pause. "She has suffered greatly here."

"Oh?" I became aware of the uneven, rocky path we were walking on.

"Everybody knows, people will tell you. The Prime Minister, his only child and daughter was taken. Near here, on the mountain there that is shared by Zimbabwe and Mozambique. The Mrs. Prime Minister and the girl were having a picnic, and the girl disappeared—just like that. It was full-sun day. Search parties looked, and some people said the RENAMO rebels stole her. But we know that it was the spirits who took her, the cost of a forbidden marriage." He stopped and pointed at the stony ridge that loomed just ahead, quiet and empty like my heart.

Shocked, I left the driver in the effort to seek out the little girl whose face so reminded me of my younger daughter's. What could I have done to protect *her*? Myself? Sensing that a thousand hungry eyes were trained on me, I stopped, clutched my cheap camera close to my body, turned slowly, and caught up with Peter. What would I have said to the girl if I had found her? How would I have introduced myself? What could I have given her that she might have wanted—I carried no cache of food, no store of grain or powdered milk? She probably didn't even speak Shona but rather some yet more distant tongue. I was relieved when Peter and I reached the relative security of the bus.

We left not much later. It was a while before anyone in the bus spoke: it had been a harrowing visit. Exhausted, we drove back to the mountains for a final night before leaving Nyanga and Zimbabwe.

At the lodge, we said goodbye to Marian Mutare, who was still talking as she was being driven away in the spotless government Mercedes. Members of my group were thinking "good riddance," though they were polite enough not to say anything.

But I shall never forget her. A person brave enough to abandon the world and the security that she grew up with and knew, a person with enough faith in herself to feel that she could become a contributing part of another culture. Her child sacrificed to a dream, the dream of human and social equality. The disappearance of the child must have occurred somewhere around the time that Rhodesia became Zimbabwe.

After that it was difficult to enjoy the cool comfort of the former Rhodes home. The anthurium looked false and foreign. The evening tea tasted bitter, its ironically natural savor. I remembered a line that the sullen anthropologist had quoted to us, something like: "I am the place where travelling occurs." And I longed for the bland landscapes of home.

Chapter Eight
Dining in Africa—A Parable

In the arid Ferlo region of Senegal, where I lived for several years, family members and visitors eat their meals together from a single large bowl placed in a shady spot under a tree or nearby awning. People gather at the call *Kai lekk*, they wash their right hands with water sprinkled from a large metal kettle, then they squat on an angle and share the food and the space of its consumption with others. An older family member pronounces a Koranic blessing for the food that is to be eaten. Dipping their hands into the bowl, the diners form palm-sized nuggets of food that they then can bring to their mouths. If the rains have failed that year, or if the family happens to be poor, the bowl will quickly empty of its grains of rice or millet pellets. Often, long before they have eaten their fill, the diners will sit back from the circle, licking the savory oil from their hands as an indication that they have finished the meal. Someone—usually the cook—asks the guests one by one why they have stopped eating. The answer is always the same: *Soor nna,* "I am not hungry." No matter the number of people gathered around the enamel bowl and no matter how hungry those people may be, the meal ends the same way: there is a portion of food left in the center of the serving dish. In this way the villagers maintain the appearance of plenty: a clean bowl would suggest that the host had not prepared enough food or, worse yet, that the host was not generous. The meal is also a demonstration of a tacit understanding among the villagers—that it is good to suppress one's individual needs for the well-being of the group. Squatting among friends and family members, the Senegalese villagers consciously curb their own appetites as they share the common food of human togetherness.

Years after my stay in Senegal, I was part of a study group that traveled to southern Africa. There were 16 of us, all academics from midwestern universities, all hungry for the "authentic" African experience. Some of us were new to the continent while others, like me, had lived and worked previously in Africa. We were funded, in part, by a grant from the United States State Department; an official document noted that one aim of the program was for us "to take in the cultures of the continent." Fed on a diet of exotic places, we were to return to our universities with new perspectives and plans for teaching. We would incorporate our new knowledge into our classes; our experiences would shape our teaching. In our grant applications, we had all convincingly made the case that our students would eventually become the beneficiaries of our intercultural largesse.

Everyone was looking for the authentic Africa. Given the remarkable geographic and social diversity of the continent, I'm not sure what might constitute that single, unadulterated authentic experience. We all had our own jaundiced learning to deal with, all those stereotypes and expectations that had accrued to our minds over the years of TV news programs and radio clips, not to mention the hours of our eclectic reading—Africans as exploited victims of international greed and contemporary neglect, Africans as quiescent but quaint social groups, Africans as corrupt innocents.

Then, too, we were all academics, all trained to look for and find rational patterns of social behavior and material manifestations of cultural activity. It didn't occur to us that, perhaps, others' behavior might not be explained with the words of our language. After all, we had learned to measure everything in economic terms; indeed, in the late twentieth century the word *progress* in English generally betokens material improvement or mere material proliferation. No one talks about spiritual progress or our progress as developing human beings; these qualities are never part of a discussion of development or, often, of culture; they do not easily figure in the connotation of the word *progress*. At the same time, it didn't occur to us that the very process of divvying up and scrutinizing others— as the great thinkers and the revered professors who taught us had done before us—presupposes that the human being, like a math problem, can be conceived as a set of systems, never greater than the sum of its constituent parts, always reducible to manageable bits that can be fairly captured in language and codified by the mind. Our higher degrees were proof of our faith in this rationality.

One member of our group—a Professor of English and a specialist in African American literature—felt that he had particular insight into African cultures since he knew the literary culture of black Americans so well. He spent a lot of time in the dim hotel bars expressing his opinions on just about any subject, speaking insistently and dramatically despite the gathering alcoholic haze. As he gained argumentative momentum, his bowl-cut hair would shake like fringe on some ancient drapery. For him, all subjects were fair game for this bantering brand of intellectual investigation; all issues could be approached and resolved with the marshaling of significant evidence in convincing verbal contexts. And all matters sooner or later related to his wide reading in literary studies and literature. He became especially excited when he made one of his "connections", when he could match up another's comment or an observation to some lived or vicarious experience of his own. The danger of this approach is that it regularly runs the risk of being reductive, of simplifying or reducing the outside world to one's limited experience. That risk was great for all of us, short-term visitors to places so different from home, all of us carrying lots of our own cultural baggage.

I think the trip must have been particularly unsatisfying for him: he seemed to be so irritated or angry most of the time. During our stay in Harare, for instance, he became especially enraged when, at a free concert given by students at the University of Zimbabwe, the students performed western pop music as well as traditional tunes done on kalimbas and drums. I remember his saying, "I didn't come to Africa to hear Beatles' music. I hope they are not doing this music for us." As it turned out, his sentiment was echoed by many others of our group. We knew that the electric guitars and 70s songs could not be part of African musical traditions; we felt that the students had cheapened what should have been a pristine musical offering by including tunes that had aired in the commercial worlds of our youth.

Nonetheless, it was embarrassing that we had given the students such tepid applause at the conclusion of the concert. They had, after all, prepared the music especially for us. It didn't occur to my colleagues that African students might hear and enjoy western music—especially pop—or that many of the University students might find themselves uncomfortable in the traditional village dress of our stereotypes.

The leader of our tour—a wise and amiable man who had spent a good deal of time in Africa—had arranged for us to spend the next several weeks in Malawi, a country where he had worked as a Fulbright lecturer. He knew the country well though he never claimed any special, insider knowledge of the Malawis. And though he knew Americans well, he never chided us for our caviling or our occasional bad manners. As he had done in Zimbabwe, he arranged for us to meet professors and professionals; we sat through lectures at the University, listened to politicians talk about structural adjustment programs, heard a licensed traditional healer speak about herbal remedies and simples. It was an informative but tiring program, rather heavy on the cognitive diet.

The schedule included a free day mid-way through our stay in Malawi. Our leader—his name was David—recommended that we take a bus trip to a rural feeding station near the Mozambique border.

"It's not more than a couple of hours' drive," he promised. "I know that it's not part of our official itinerary, but this should be a unique experience. There are many Mozambique refugees in the area," he added, no doubt aware that the word *refugee* would pique our interest.

As professionals, we expected to have a rationale for everything we did; it was part of our training—some sort of justification or the promise of some tangible product that might result from a given experience. David knew that he should ask. Now that I think about it, I see that there was a subtle urgency to his asking. He explained that the villagers would be waiting for us in the late morning and that we would only stay long enough to observe the daily distribution of gruel and pay respects to the villagers. We would be back in plenty of time to gather at the fancy Chinese restaurant in Blantyre for a farewell dinner, our goodbye to Malawi and to Africa. Everything was in place, waiting for us; we would even be fêted at the conclusion of the long day. How could we refuse?

At the time we were set up in a faded but pleasant hotel in Blantyre and had to weigh the prospect of a jostling bus ride into the bush against the modest comforts of the hotel. We could have sat in the bar with its wooden tables darkened by shoe polish mirroring the stuffed game trophies that hung from the walls. Yet most of us were both horrified and intrigued at the possibility of visiting a refugee camp—not to mention witnessing the feeding program. Not surprisingly, perhaps, all my colleagues agreed to take the trip.

We knew enough history to know that Mozambique had been at war within itself for years—actively ever since the Portuguese had pulled out in 1975, passively ever since the colonizers had claimed African land for themselves so many years before that.

The Portuguese approach to imperialism was so unlike that of the British and the French, who became inextricably involved in internal politics and in the economic destinies of their colonies. Never really a part of the new-world order of the late twentieth century, the Portuguese maintained distant and feudal control of their possessions. In Mozambique, the Portuguese did little to improve transportation or communication within the country. Few roads, schools, or other institutions were built in the hundreds of years that Portugal thought of itself as Mozambique's "mother country." Effective imperialists, the Portuguese learned to disguise grisly mercantile motives by couching them in the discourse of family supportiveness and care: on the level of rhetoric, the attachment between the small European nation and this sprawling tropical expanse along the southeast coast of Africa was expressed in terms of mother and child. All the while, the Portuguese extracted large profits from the lucrative shrimp catch and big revenues from the railroad lines that connected the Portuguese coast with the English and French colonies of the interior. The tiny mother country—whose empire and claim to international grand-standing has long ago vanished—had discovered the value of using its children as chattel.

Meanwhile, professional and managerial positions were held by expatriates or other Europeans while the Mozambican population provided a plentiful source of cheap labor for local colonial enterprises and, when those began to dry up, for South African mines and fields. So when the Portuguese pulled out once and for all in 1975, they left a country with little infrastructure, lots of debt, and great social and economic turmoil—the final gift of their colonial parenthood.

At the time, South Africa played an active though spectral hand in the internal instability of many nations of southern Africa. The avowedly racist government in Pretoria felt it had a moral imperative to extirpate what it determined to be inimical to its economic and political health—even when that meant interfering in the internal affairs of other, sovereign nations. Funding and training for RENAMO, the Mozambican National Resistance, came from South Africa, which shares a border with Mozambique. For years, rebels from RENAMO led a guerrilla war against the government of Mozambique. To be sure, RENAMO had been the brainchild of members of the white settler regime in Zimbabwe, afraid for the loss of their regional political power and material wealth, likewise fearful of the incursion of socialism in their ideological and physical backyard. But in the 1970s, the white settlers in Zimbabwe were fighting their own civil war to maintain hegemony, and South Africa decided to take matters into its own hands.

The Mozambican government would have had its hands full without internal, guerrilla war. But things got worse. The monsoon winds that blow down the Mozambique Channel failed to collect their typical torrents of rain for four years running, and the resultant droughts from 1981 to 1984 decimated food production and reduced much of the population to gaunt figures teeming at one relief station or another. We had seen the coverage on the nightly news; churches appealed to us to give money to help with relief efforts. As crops in one part of the country failed, the people—tied down with few possessions—began to move. Together, the drought and the political instability resulted in large numbers of hungry and displaced peopled. Already hard-pressed to feed their own populations, neighboring Malawi and Zimbabwe have had to deal with an undetermined but enormous influx of Mozambicans, not to mention regular border raids by bands of RENAMO rebels.

It was the summer of 1993 that we visited the western borders—farthest from the sea—of this nation not yet 20 years old. Inside the country, RENAMO attacks were frequent and fierce; the economy was in a shambles. At the time, no law held in Mozambique; almost no governmental institution functioned. I had lived in places where mail rarely arrived and where letters would show up months past the postmark broken open and bearing the grime of someone else's reading. I had lived in places where shelves in local shops sat empty for months, waiting for canned goods that could not enter the country because the currency had been devalued again or the port had been on strike. I had lived in places where political elections meant curfews and street warfare for months both before and after the purportedly democratic event. Yet, in 1993, conditions in Mozambique must have been so much worse. No roads were safe for travel, few air or river routes were clear. What little there was in the way of educational and health infrastructure had disintegrated. People were starving.

We jounced our way to a meeting with some of these people. The trip started pleasantly enough: the 18-seat Mercedes bus left Blantyre and the highlands early in the winter day, but we soon came down to the level of the Shire River, only a few hundred feet above sea level, hot and sticky. The driver, whose English was not good, managed to make us understand that the paved road that we were following had been built by the Zimbabweans, though I am sure he said *Rhodesians*. Soon enough, we jerked off the road and followed a dirt track that ran through fields and dry creeks as it made its way from village to village and an eventual rendezvous with the Mozambique border.

One member of our group was angry that the trip was taking so long. She was a specialist in modern Europe, in countries whose material prosperity and competitiveness have been so great that recent history has become, largely, a chronicle of their rivalry in the form of increasingly catastrophic wars.

"You told us it would only be three more kilometers," she said to the driver, who spent much of the trip talking vigorously to his companion.

"Only three kilometers," he would repeat, smiling, as the kilometers clicked off. "Only three kilometers!" Getting no satisfaction from the driver, the woman turned on David.

"Why are we being taken on this wild goose chase?" she demanded. "Some of us would have stayed back at the hotel if we had known the drive would be this long. And so damn unpleasant."

By this time, the bus was pretty much coated with dust, and the temperature outside must have been close to 100 degrees.

To pacify her, our guide suggested that we eat the lunch that had been prepared for us by the hotel kitchen. It was well past noon, and the bottles of Coke and Fanta had long since warmed to bus temperature. David reasoned that the food might be a welcome diversion from the uncomfortable ride.

The driver chose that moment to interject "just three more kilometers," which, I was happy to see, the Professor of History did not take as sarcasm. She relented, and we agreed that we would eat as we lurched along, saving time if not abetting digestion. The driver slowed long enough for two people to grab the boxes of provisions at the back of the bus. Sadly for us, the cooks had included fried chicken in our lunch, imagining, I am sure, that the chicken would be a pleasant reminder of stateside cuisine. I can still see a drumstick as it slipped from the greased lips of a bus passenger as we hit a dip in the road. Most of us chose to let the chicken rest in its hot packing at the back of the bus, selecting pieces of fruit and warm soda instead.

By this time the worn path we had been following had disintegrated into the irregular tufts of grass that cover the savannah in this dry part of Malawi. Few vehicles had preceded us on this trip. We didn't know that we were very close to the Mozambique border. There, the grass and occasional trees carry on for great distances that are broken only by rare, deserted villages—the look of poverty in a lawless country.

At first we could just barely hear the music—drums and hand-clapping. At the sound of the singing, the sociologist in the group jumped to the window with his camcorder. Like a contemporary Cyclops, he spent a good deal of the trip leaning out of bus windows, the monocular machine strapped to his shoulder gathering footage and, he hoped, material for an article or two. "This place is great!" he announced. The bus was approaching the village.

By the time the bus had come to rest inside the collection of a couple of dozen or so huts, the villagers had gathered round. They were pointing, laughing, singing, dancing. Women with infants strapped to their backs, their heads swathed in bright cloths; barefoot kids; tall men hanging back near the great tree that served as village center. Just beyond the tree and outside of its circle of broken shade, a few bony cattle were corralled.

We wiped grease from our hands and faces, smoothed our clothes, and prepared for the meal we had come so far to witness.

"They sing welcome to you," the driver explained. "They thank you." As we disembarked, we snatched our cameras and began snapping the brilliant faces and the spectacular dances. The sociologist was in his element—visual and auditory stimulus in all directions at once. He would be able to make a multi-sensational record of the event, a sort of African village *son et lumière*.

Several of us felt a little uncomfortable photographing the event of which we were so much a part. This was an event we had initiated by our incursion into the lives of these people. And rather than participate, all we could do was photograph them. In addition, there seemed something perverse about our hunger for photos and memorabilia as we prepared our future records of the moment. It seemed to me that our desire for material evidence of our experience interfered with our actually being present in that moment in that village. But we were, after all, academics, those whose lives are given to the analysis of written records, the two-dimensional artifacts of lived life.

A man came forward and, with a wave of his hand, put an end to the dances and the songs. He was a government nurse, he explained to us, and wanted to show us how successful the feeding project had been. We followed him to a hut, no large than six feet square, where he pointed to an open ledger on top of a wooden desk, his work table. Someone had carefully entered the date, the amount of gruel prepared, and the number of women fed. The records went on for pages and pages, all in the same flowery script from the nib of a quill pen. Villagers—mostly children—gathered just at the fringes of our group as we peered into the official hut; they kept just a couple of feet between themselves and us, though they stood right up against one another, many holding hands or leaning on the shoulder of another.

Amoeba-like, we backed out of the hut in time for the feeding to begin. A group of about 50 women was gathered beneath the palaver tree. They sat in the dirt, their skirts swirling around them in bolts of bright color. Each woman held an infant close; some were breastfeeding while others rocked their child from side to side. It was beautiful. Was it pride that we read on their faces, smiling there? I cannot know, but the feeding that July day became a ceremony in that border village. The center of everyone's attention, the women were smiling quietly.

I was happy to see that promoters of the feeding program had learned from the mistakes of the baby-formula campaigns of the 60s and 70s. That commercial campaign to sell modernization along with baby formula was so successful in Africa that many women—with access to neither clean water nor the means for sterilization—felt that bottle feeding had to be better than breast feeding and so stopped feeding their children their naturally clean and healthful breast milk in favor of plying the kids with the diluted products of cans of powdered pap that many could scarcely afford. The result was a generation of infants that died horribly from dysentery or other diseases related to poor sanitation.

This program, on the other hand, encouraged breast-feeding and fed the mothers, the givers of milk. As the women were seated, nursing their children, the nurse and his co-workers spread out among them with bowls of high-protein gruel. Children up to the age of four or five could also eat, and many of these kids sat in front of us in the sandy dirt slurping their gruel. Just outside the inner circle stood the *other* children, those who had survived to age six or eight, those whose relative well-being prevented their being included in the banquet that warm afternoon. They stood quiet and rigid watching us and the others. It did not take much to imagine what they might have been feeling as they stood there hungry, outside of our circle of foreign opulence and outside of the circle of favored local people.

The feeding did not take long, and the nurse was back tallying up his numbers by the time the singing and dancing resumed. We didn't need the driver to help us understand that the villagers were thanking us for the food, attributing the limited gift to us. Some of us were embarrassed.

We asked the nurse how the confusion had come to be. The nurse told us that the feeding program had been initiated years before by an American church. Large burlap sacks of food labeled in bold letters "Gift of the United States" regularly found their way to the village; Mozambican church officials came from time to time to oversee the distribution of the food. With a slightly inflated air, the nurse announced: "The Baptists care about us."

David took a few of us aside and quietly emended the nurse's commentary. David told us that the Baptists had withdrawn their funding of the feeding program when they discovered that Mozambique was a socialist country. It had, apparently, taken a number of years for the news of the African nation's swing to the left to reach the American churchgoers. Unable to stomach any support for people on the other column of the ideological menu, the Baptists cut their funding and withheld their food—waiting for more ideologically amenable hungry people to come along.

"Surprisingly," David continued, "it is an organization in South Africa that has taken over the support of the feeding program." He paused for us to fully realize the strange irony. "South Africa is full of contradictions, you know. Despite some terrible conditions of oppression, there are many wonderful people working for significant change and justice."

And the villagers were crediting us with their good fortune. I looked at the women feeding their infants in that dappled shade. I imagined the women wielding hammers or rifles, inflicting Marxism on a world of complacent capitalists. I imagined these displaced, hungry women running a propaganda campaign shouting slogans in a European language they didn't even know to a population too close to the land and their traditions to know or care about ideology. I imagined these people to be my enemies. And those enemies were thanking me now.

We stayed only a few moments longer. The cheers and dances increased as we made our way to the bus. We went for our seats and, like the sociologist, we all leaned out the windows, waving as we headed away from our hosts. Soon, the noises of the bounding bus supplanted cheers and sounds from the village; we all sat silent. None of us spoke during the return trip, and there were no complaints about the ride or the driving. Even the young anthropologist—who had been quite vocal on the tour, always providing paradigms for what he felt he had seen or what we should have seen—did not attempt to interpret for us.

Back in Blantyre, we had a little time to get ready at the hotel before we were to take taxis to the Chinese restaurant for our final meal and meeting. I shared the taxi ride with an African American Professor of Education. She had become rather unpopular among the members of the group mostly because she regularly reminded the others of us that only she "could truly understand the Africans" we met since only she had experienced life's tragedies as deeply as they. She felt that her color—not shared culture or language or beliefs—gave her an automatic empathy and understanding that none of us could ever attain. And it was impossible to argue with her position: she simply retorted that anyone whose opinion differed from hers was racist and therefore wrong. Her position assumed that tacit understanding is shared among members of a group, though I doubt that any of our African hosts would have included the Professor of Education—educated, overweight, outspoken, and American—in any intimate circles of their own.

A small incident in the cab displayed the limits of her "understanding." We had selected a cab from among the many that were stationed in front of the hotel. The driver understood little English and looked very nervous as we climbed into the back seat. He hurtled us through town in his rickety car, casting glances back into the back seat as the Professor of Education was exclaiming her understanding of the day's events. "It must have been a white church," she deduced, thereby reducing a serious cultural and inter-cultural problem to a racialist one. "No black church would abandon its brothers and sisters like that." As she continued the profession of her knowledge, she extended her large hands to the front and grabbed the driver's back as she announced:

"I know what's best for you, honey! You look so tense to me. Mama knows what's best. Just let Mama do her thing." With that announcement, she began vigorously massaging the narrow back and thin neck of the driver.

With the first grip, the driver lurched forward, and the taxi, already unstable, swerved at an oncoming ox cart filled with tobacco leaves. The driver shrank forward just outside her reach; he became even more agitated and nervous. She made another grab, and this time caught a shoulder blade, pressing her hand into his back and neck. The bizarre little dance continued until we reached the restaurant, which thankfully wasn't far.

We arrived safe but shaken, and I put a whole stack of Malawi kwachas in the driver's hand. I had barely managed to retract my arm from the open window when he slammed the car into reverse and rushed off. So much for intercultural exchange. The cart and its tobacco survived, but I think that our driver may not soon get over the unprovoked encounter from the rear. Unaware of local custom and ignorant of local language, the Professor of Education insisted on prosecuting her massage. I did not think that she knew "what was best" for the driver—whose language and culture were so different from hers—despite the understanding that she assumed.

We got to the restaurant safely and began our feast. Since the rate of exchange was so favorable to the American dollar, we ordered extravagantly. Great plates of steaming food arrived at our tables; the servers carried the plates ceremoniously from guest to guest. Like respectful visitors in a Senegalese village, we left great mounds of uneaten food, but for a different reason. We were all already well-fed. We had only ourselves, individually, to look after; we owed nothing to our fellow travelers.

Like the Mozambican women, we had eaten, but we had already been fed by the predispositions that come along with an educational system that accepts that the manifest world can be chopped up into distinguishable bits that language can passively classify in a rational way. This is the sort of knowledge that we can consume as food—acquaintance with things and their constituent qualities. But others may conceive of qualities differently. Surely the expression *eating one's fill* does not find its way into a Wolof sentence, nor could the Mozambican women speak of *home* or *government* the same way we do. Though rationalists would like to imagine that all languages share similar categories for words and concepts, other thinkers have shown that the classificatory systems of language themselves shape our thoughts. So, to some degree, we are created by the language that we claim to control. And we are mistaken to imagine that, through the careful administration of language, we can achieve some sort of objective statement—and understanding—of others without a niggling questioning of our own assumptions and predispositions.

What was authentic in our experiences? Our pictures of those women feeding their infants? Our images of the villagers dancing? What of their experiences had we tasted? All of us have so long ago forgotten—if we ever had known—the feel of hunger and the still ache of want. We have also forgotten the exhilaration that the fulfilling of basic needs can provide, an exhilaration that bursts into song or dance. We share with the Baptists a culture that, to some degree, determines what we see: in our papers and lectures we can divide the world into ideological blocks, though most Mozambicans are surely not Marxist just as they could scarcely be called capitalists. Yet we demand of them—as of ourselves and our students—an affiliation, an identifying connection. And we assume that our considered experience can by extension subsume others' life experiences.

We stayed late at the restaurant, savoring shared moments from the days we had spent in Africa before returning to our hotel and our insatiable dreams.

Chapter Nine
Out of Country

The health guidebook for State Department diplomats notes that, for newcomers, a feeling of frustration and even mild depression (the French say that they feel *dépaysés*, "out-of-country") often follows an initial period of excitement and activity that accompany the discovery of unexpected pleasures and the overcoming of challenges in the new, adopted home. Though I wouldn't dream of promoting myself to the level of diplomats, I might make a similar observation about myself. My story begins with a story about Cameroon in a year of national elections in both Cameroon and the US.

In 2004 a group of ex-Congressmen from the US came to Cameroon as self-appointed election monitors during the recent presidential elections here. Elderly, courtly, and clueless, the men blew into the country and made numerous fawning appearances on local television, praising the Cameroonians for their fair and open elections and for this fine demonstration that democracy thrives in at least one African nation. The men all wore colorful ties and smiles; they shook hands vigorously everywhere the camera went; television announcers explained casually that most of them hailed from southern states, which might well have provided a primer in non-democratic politics for the ex-lawmakers. Though I didn't follow the particulars of their visit, they could not have stayed long enough to travel much into the anglophone Northwest Province, where opposition to the Cameroonian Life President has been strong and long-standing and where reports of vote fraud have been relatively consistent. Nor could they have traveled to the extreme-north, where the heat and the difficult weather conditions would surely have withered the elderly statesmen. And, as we all knew he would, the President became the President again.

Most of the international workers I have met—economists and agronomists from GDZ, the German Development Cooperation; health professionals with WHO and Red Cross—claim that Cameroon is one of the most corrupt of countries anywhere. Everyone is on the take; everyone can be bought. A

NIGER

CHAD

NIGERIA

Bénoué River

Ngaoundéré

CAMEROON

Kumbo ●● Njavnyuy
● Bamenda

● Bafoussam

CENTRAL
AFRICAN
REPUBLIC

Sanaga River

Mt Cameroon

Douala

◉ Yaoundé

*GULF OF
GUINEA*

Kribi

Lobé River

EQUATORIAL
GUINEA

GABON

REPUBLIC OF
THE CONGO

0 50 100 150 km

0 25 50 75 100 mi

prominent minister quipped to a German friend that he was angry with the Americans for keeping their project moneys off-shore and therefore out of the grasp of people who already, like the minister, lead lives of unrivalled luxury and (perhaps not entirely) unbridled power. Another important official— entrusted democratically with power to act on behalf of the people—clear-cut thousands of hectares of timber, the profits from which went directly into his bank account, people and environment be damned.

And yet even the more believable UN elections observers credited Camer- oon with reasonably fair elections and transparent voting procedures. That the social order might be foul is also transparent. And the Big Man whose local pal- ace looks down on our section of the city, who owns estates in several European countries, who spends much more time elsewhere than in his needy home coun- try—in the country whose patrimony he has appropriated for himself—that same Big Man won the elections fair and square. And I am to stand up and cheer for the triumph of a young democracy.

But then, on the other hand, what represents democratic America? What be- tokens the fruits of equal opportunity and free enterprise?

The American Embassy hunkers down just outside beat-up downtown Yaoundé, a log-jam of barricades, closed streets, concrete blocks, checkpoints, and strips of six-inch metal spikes. The interior of the building is scarcely less intimidating: razor wire adorns windows, and the guards frisked me and Jill each time we entered the compound for the first six weeks of our "welcome" to the country. The attitude of the employees is no less confrontational: Americans have told us never to travel with Cameroonians, never to leave our vehicles un- attended (we don't have one to attend), never to go to certain parts of the city. As newly-arrived and therefore apparently idiotic expatriates, we were made to sit through a security briefing where the many military features of the Embassy and of expatriate life in Cameroon were extolled, our protection from "the bad guys," as the pleasant but frightening officer explained, provided as rationale for the offensive posture that we ought well to adopt here.

Then there are the diplomats themselves, a professional cadre charged with representing the US elsewhere and promulgating its values.

My family—daughters Johanna and Mollie and my wife Jill—and I arrived in Cameroon a day before the new ambassador came to town. Since then I have learned that the new head of the Embassy here is kind and approachable (few that I have met have been so willing to talk to those of us outside of the magic circle of the *corps diplomatique*) and an ex-Peace Corps volunteer, and he and his family live in a spectacular mansion that, as you might imagine, resides in the *quartier* of spectacular mansions. I admit that I much enjoyed the evening I spent on the verandah of that house—lounging in a soft chair on the screened-in porch done in cream and green under lazy ceiling fans, sipping a regularly re- plenished cold drink, looking out over a well-managed lawn (in a climate and soil rather inimical to the growing of grass) and thriving garden where the fam- ily dogs were playing, happily unaware that they live better than many people in this city. I particularly admired the garden, a series of raised beds filled with the marvelous botanical treasures of this rich country—heliconias, frangipani, hibiscus, philodendron—delimited by allées of durian, mango, and ravinala trees. That evening, our hosts credited the vegetable brilliance of the garden to the work of the wife of the previous ambassador though I feel certain that she never touched a plant or lifted a spadeful of soil in that space. Unnamed gardeners had soiled themselves with that work, and the beneficent climate made fantastic, fruitful contributions to their toil. The subject of conversation then turned away from the garden, and, like a conscientious hostess, the ambassador's wife began describing to the ladies how she had planned to redo the cavernous living room, sending to the States for fabrics and wall coverings in order to make the palace more "livable" and to her individual taste.

Once, as we were kept waiting outside the home of the ambassador's assistant as the guard flipped nervously through pages of those on the guest list of a party to which we had been invited, I imagined what it must be like for most Cameroonians almost all the time: lingering outside institutions to which they may never gain admission while they witness others coming and going, fancy vehicles delivering acceptable visitors to an Emerald City whose architectural details they may barely discern behind walls that are at once concealing and alluring. Except that the Cameroonians would likely not have been invited.

What would an ordinary Cameroonian, with visions of chauffeured land-rovers that shuttle diplomats from covered bunker to enclosed paradise, come to think of the place that produced such people and life-styles? What developmental lessons in democracy could come from the vision of a world untouchably rich and removed?

On tables in the beautiful library of the American School of Yaoundé, books written by Africans sit splayed open, inviting young readers to taste and ingest. Novels of Chinua Achebe, an anthology of women's poetry from African countries, translations of francophone novels of Cameroonians Mongo Beti and Ferdinand Oyono. The books haven't moved much since I have been around. Last week I picked up Nelson Mandela's *No Easy Walk to Freedom*, blew off the dust, riffled the pages, and found these words:

> The structure and organization of early African societies . . . fascinated me . . . The land, then the main means of production, belonged to the whole tribe, and there was no individual ownership whatsoever. There were no classes, no rich or poor and no exploitation of man by man. All men were free and equal and this was the foundation of government. Recognition of this general principle found expression in the constitution of the council, . . . which governs the affairs of the tribe . . . Chief and subject, warrior and medicine man, all took part.
>
> There was much in such a society that was primitive and insecure and it certainly could never measure up to the demands of the present epoch. But in such a society are contained the seeds of revolutionary democracy in which none will be held in slavery or servitude, and in which poverty, want, and insecurity shall be no more. This . . . inspires me and my colleagues in our political struggle.[1]

These stirring words were spoken in an open court—whose self-conscious justices undoubtedly drove home later that night to spacious villas surrounded by layers of whatever security measures were deemed appropriate at the time— just before Mandela was whisked off to Robben Island and to the secure interior of the social prison he had tried so hard to dismantle as an active member of a non-democratic world.

Of course, Bush supporters would quickly say, the world *has* improved— and Mandela's release, summary ascension to leadership in South Africa, and continued impact throughout the world all assent to the melioration of national behavior—even in poor countries (though Bush might have trouble remembering the name of Mandela's country or its leaders). And, they would add, democracy can grow in such soils.

I have read Tom Paine—and with more than literary enthusiasm—and I do believe that societies can always be more just and that democracy, as an ideal, can exist, if only as incentive for the improvement of current conditions.

Though not, perhaps, in this world.

Today, I am very worried about the distance between the honeyed sound of our words and the arrogant force of our example. I am worried about religious demagoguery that masks itself as righteous concern for others or as justification for seeking violent revenge. I am worried about leaders of a self-declared democracy who trump up a war, then complain when self-respecting nations of the world do not support that war and when a world witnesses with horror the continued carnage of that war.

Dépaysé, I guess I am worried about the outcome of the presidential election in my own country. Whoever wins, the triumph of wealth over wealth will hardly be democratic.

NOTES

1. Mandela, Nelson. *No Easy Walk to Freedom*. London: Heinemann, 1978. pp. 147-8.

Chapter Ten

The Dark of Heartlessness

From the open ocean, dirty surf flushes up to the beaches, boomerang stretches of brown sand broken here and there by outcrops of darker-brown rock. Even on clear days, the sea seems murky gray, its rhythmic churning rarely if ever resulting in the apparent cleansing of the water.

The shore, on the other hand, leans towards the water as if beckoning to its passengers. Twisted and contorted from some vegetable knowledge of optimal growing conditions in a crowded environment, coconut palms assume unlikely curved shapes for trees; their fronds spurt fountain-like from the humped trunks that support freeloading colonies of green plants, epiphytes and ferns. Before the palms drop their fruit, local children will have clambered up, grabbed the globes, and hacked a free snack. Pressing in on the palms from both sides, thick-leaved evergreen trees clutch to the receding western edge of the continent with penetrating tangles of root-anchors, sometimes almost entirely exposed by vagrant tides, a web of earth-bound support. As if in procession, these brilliant trees follow the coast, the salt-spray no intimidation to their vigorous growth.

Following this coastline towards the equator, you will soon come upon a flashy waterfall, what people here musically call "les chutes de la Lobé." The nodding palms and shimmering broadleaf evergreen trees give way for the space of about 300 feet, and the Lobé River pours its turbid charge—carried from rain-soaked forests hundreds of miles into the interior of the continent and across an invisible equator—into the Atlantic Ocean. The river drops about 30 feet through a filter of rocks and tiny islands of plants that may rejoice in the fresh water but also appear fearful of the destructive possibilities of its fierce falling. Just beyond the sucking sounds and dangerous currents of the falls, the Lobé flows hot, quiet, and slow between thick banks of vegetable growth. This was the river we took into the heart of this country.

From the vantage point of a ship in the open ocean, perhaps, this coastline might appear unchanged from what Joseph Conrad and others might have seen a hundred or so years ago. Mile after mile of social palms interspersed with huddling broad-leaved trees, the front line for an interior of yet more steamy green. Conrad would have cruised by en route to the mouth of the Congo, not too far down the Atlantic coast from the Lobé. Though smaller in volume and discharge, what other rivers might have taken Conrad into the interior of this enormous and astonishingly various land? Ironically, the Congo River that on the maps looks like a great coiled snake provided Europeans with their access, however fabled and fraught with difficulty, into the heart of the continent as well as a metaphor for the grave danger of material enticements.

History—at least the history of the encounters of local peoples with Europeans—may have been kinder to the people of this region, Cameroon and Equatorial Guinea, than it was to those who may have watched Conrad's ships steam by. From *King Leopold's Ghost* we now know (but had for at least 100 years insisted on disremembering, for the crimes perpetrated in the Belgian Congo were international headlines in the early years of the twentieth century) that 10,000,000 people or more[1]—possibly one-half of the entire population at the time—perished as the Belgians prosecuted their imperial assault on the peoples of that other river, chain-ganging Africans to rip rubber and yank ivory from a colonial possession more than 75 times the size of the minute metropolitan nation jammed in the low, flat northwest corner of Europe. As Conrad makes clear in his famous tale *Heart of Darkness*—published in 1899, just after the European grab for African land had begun in organized earnest—the encounters of Europe and Africa were seldom without material cost to Africans and, as Conrad describes, moral challenge to thoughtful Europeans.

But, before his turn inward at the Congo, Conrad would surely not have noticed the string of hotels that hide in coves along the more appealing beaches of what is now the country of Cameroon. Interestingly, one of the most luxurious of the hotels, the Ilomba, is itself the most unapproachable, hidden, as it is, at the terminus of a deeply rutted dirt lane—flecked on both sides by small wattle or gray cinderblock Cameroonian houses—scarcely navigable by anything but four-wheel drive vehicles or the sure passage of local feet. Bumping along the unpaved road that rides the drenched coast south into Equatorial Guinea, you know the location of the turn-off to this hotel by the presence of a pink Pentecostal church that shares the corner with a water tower. A square block Jehovah's Witness meetinghouse looks on from across the red-cinder track. If Conrad missed this stopping-off point, other westerners have not. As you turn off the road and drive towards the Ilomba hotel, you leave fundamentalist Christianity behind. You might stop and enjoy the beach at the hotel with its charming thatched-roof bar that luxuriates just outside the splash of the biggest waves. A coconut's throw down the beach, Cameroonian fishermen sit in their stranded pirogues and repair their nets. If Conrad and his crew were to pass by today, blacks and whites alike might take note.

My family and I visited this beach paradise in November 2004. We did not stay in the fancy resort, opting for a cheaper hotel closer to the town of Kribi. A young Cameroonian came to the hotel one morning, advertising a privately shepherded trip up the Lobé River to see the Pygmy villages. Immediately I said

Yes, knowing that my daughters Johanna, 16, and Mollie, 14, would be excited by the trip. It would be one of those *de rigueur* African experiences. I listened. As he talked price, I began to think about the cost of our interruption of the lives of people whom we did not know and who probably did not want to know us. An academic trained to recoil at the uttering of the politically incorrect, I remembered that the official name of the ethnic group is *Baka* and knew that the more familiar word *Pygmy* recalled unflattering stereotypes. The man and I settled for a pirogue ride up the Lobé, no stopover for a visit to the Baka, at a reduced rate.

By the time the morning came, I had reconsidered. Partly because I watched Johanna's face light up at the mention of the Pygmies. Partly because our driver, Richard, a Cameroonian from the mountainous northwestern part of the country, *really* wanted to see Pygmies (Richard had never heard of the word *Baka*.) Mine was a minority position, and I gave in: we would visit the Pygmies and sweat our way up the river.

Like Conrad, we had to portage to reach the interior, highland reaches of the river. Except that we accomplished most of that travel in a small Toyota taxi, jouncing along grassy tracks through villages of mud-and-wattle homes, one-story rectangles with corrugated tin roofs. We bounced to a stop on a little rise and disembarked. Sticky warm morning, bright though hazy sun, little breeze. Through a field thick with cocoyams and manioc stalks, we walked about a hundred yards over and down the slight hill. It was as if we had stepped into another environment or, as Conrad says, "back in time."

Suddenly, the forest rose up to meet us, huge trees hunching around the still estuary that, nearby, held several 12-foot pirogues all made of inch-thick wood planks lashed together with sutures of metal splashed with tar. From the trees, vines hung thick, creating panels of living green that stretched from the solid branches into the dark water. Oversized ferns sprouted from the spongy banks. A few birds—dull gray ones—skittered in the mud near the boats; spider webs spun between branches in the trees. Otherwise, there was little apparent animal life. No somnolent alligators or hoped-for hippos. We stepped gingerly into the boat, settled onto a plank, breathed deeply. The guide pushed off, and we slid into the river.

Not far from shore we glided past foundation stones of what must have been a bridge. Three equal-sized pylons of stacked stone set at regular intervals. Our guide told us that the stonework was all that remained of the local efforts of Germans in their relatively small role in the scramble for Africa. I recalled my history: the Germans *had* been in this region; Cameroon's first colonial name was *Kamerun*; the Germans had planted themselves firmly farther to the north along the sea. Not unlike what Conrad witnessed in the cruel Belgian management of its gigantic colony nearby, the Germans were known for their harsh treatment of local peoples in this place. And maybe a small-scale enactment of the enslavement of locals that Conrad records took place right in this spot. But, unlike the Belgian Congo, it was external political events—not the explosion of the country from within—that drove the Germans away. Part of the price of defeat that they paid at the end of the Great War was their African colonial empire. Spoils of an alien war, Kamerun was divided into British Cameroon and French Cameroun and for many years maintained a sort of schizophrenic national identity; you can still find atlases that refer to the country as The Cameroons. Yet, evidence of German self-interest can still be seen, though the remains of the bridge now carry only ferns and support branches of climax trees. The forest has done its best to reclaim its space.

Though the estuary was preternaturally dark and quiet, it was not frightening—to me or to the girls—as I might have expected. In fact, I was hoping that we might spend more time dodging enormous boles and ducking under drapes of liana before emerging into the open river, the appeal of the surrounding natural quiet was so great. But we reached the wide water in ten or fifteen minutes. The guide paddled us out into the Lobé River; the sun took over.

With the promise of Pygmies still on the guide's lips (he too had never heard of the name *Baka*), we reached what for me would become the greatest part of our adventure—gliding down a tropical river with its gallery forest intact. Having taught Conrad's story to countless groups of students, I have always marveled at the paragraph that describes the narrator's first sustained reaction to the flora of the upper reaches of the Congo:

> "Going up that river was like travelling back to the earliest beginnings of the world, when vegetation rioted on the earth and the big trees were kings. An empty stream, a great silence, an impenetrable forest. The air was warm, thick, heavy, sluggish. There was no joy in the brilliance of sunshine. The long stretches of the waterway ran on, deserted, into the gloom of overshadowed distances."[2]

In a climate constantly warm and with annual rainfall at Kribi well in excess of 100 inches, the vegetation does riot, and the trees grow major-majestic, the greatest ones lifting their typically airy branches far above the thicker forest that hunkers close to earth. And the air is always thick, tangibly humid, steamed by early-morning sun into a solid air-borne shower. Once up above the protective canopy, the sun here burns more intensely and more dangerously than in its timid European or northern American manifestations. Pale northern complexions quickly burn without the protection of hats and skin creams.

But this stream is scarcely empty, nor is the surrounding forest. Little clearings by the river's edge reveal collections of small woven baskets used to snag fresh-water shrimp, plentiful in these waters. The baskets are attached by little grassy thongs to reeds or bushes just above the water's reach and within the grasp of local fishermen. Mollie noticed a number of places where the undergrowth at the river's edge opened up enough to reveal a network of footpaths that veered off in several directions. At one such junction, a large scaffolding of sticks had been constructed; the guide told us it was a monkey snare. And the river itself curls around islets, eddies and gurgles, rushes around inundated shrubs or laps against big rocks. Tiny, beautiful African Pygmy Kingfishers, crowned blue with brilliant orange breasts and a cerulean mantle, sit still on tree branches unaware of our passing; they suddenly dive, their sharp pointed bills flashing into the water and out again with a fish or insect. And all the time we are on the water, occasional shrieks—monkeys or jungle cats?—pierce the permanently humid air. This place is not empty, it is very much alive, and that life need not be inimical to humans, as Conrad implies.

We had paddled upstream for more than an hour when the guide suddenly directed the pirogue straight across the river, pushing against a strong current to keep us pointed upstream still. The girls saw where we were heading—an opening in the greenery beneath an overhang of tree branches. We slid into a slot on the bank, disembarked, and climbed about ten feet up the slippery soil. Then the forest took over, and well-worn paths headed off in several directions. We followed our guide into the relative dark.

Though there had been no rain for a couple of days, the paths were wet and puddled. I slipped a couple of times, and we all slogged through one particularly gooey spot, our plastic sandals making sucking sounds as they popped free of the mud. I was surprised to find that forest—the geographers label it a Guinea-equatorial type—similar to boreal forests of my home in mid-western United States: stretches of dappled sunlight with lots of shrubby plants crowding the path; then, darker sections where the major trees take over and the forest floor opens up a little. It was familiar and new at once but never foreboding. Was I wrong to interpret the signs of this place in the vocabulary of my own experience, one whose green markers include tall climax oaks and broad maples, undergrowth greenbrier and brambles? Was I wrong *not* to look for what Conrad labels a "vengeful aspect" in the brute beauty of this natural environment?

A few sentences later in Conrad's story comes the following observation: "And this stillness of life did not in the least resemble a peace. It was the stillness of an implacable force brooding over an inscrutable intention."[3] Attributing intention—inscrutable or not—to a forest or a river or even to the "force" that animates that forest has always seemed absurd to me. I wonder if Conrad had projected his bad conscience onto an impassive world, this tropical forest so vitally different from the thinned woods of northern Europe that were hacked into serviceable submission years before the push into Africa in search of "raw materials." Conrad was, after all, part of an imperial mission into the Congo, and he was aware of the cruel treatment of Africans at the hands of Europeans who, ironically, were often fêted and lauded at home, in comfortable and distant European capital cities. And then I thought of Hawthorne and the Puritan world he so convincingly describes where "nature," depicted typically dark and insidious, is the site of forbidden human activities and the perverse temple of antisocial behavior. I wonder if—as others have suggested—the west fears and then unconsciously inculpates the natural world in part to justify its rituals of conquest and submission.

Suddenly, the guide made a series of sharp hooting noises—*ou, ou, ou, ou*—and Conrad ran off. Then, from out ahead of us, a response. *Ou, ou, ou, ou.* We had all seen enough television to know without understanding that we were approaching the Pygmies' village and that our guide was announcing our coming. Richard smiled with approval. Mollie and I scraped mud from our legs and shorts. The forest cover quickly broke up, and the clear forest path became a bed of trampled grass. Bananas bunched off to one side; on the other, manioc grew intentionally tall among burned-out stumps of trees. We passed a tiny thatched hut, no more than five-feet high, framed in sticks and subdivided into minute rooms, all empty. We walked on. Another hut, and another. We were there.

And there *they* were. Not as short as we might have imagined, the men were gathered together in front of a couple of thatched lean-tos. Dressed in western-style T-shirts and loincloths, they were smoking cigarettes and passing a bottle around. About 12 men in all: a few sat on wooden stools; a couple of them squatted on the ground; several stood behind, the tallest still shorter by far than Mollie's 5'4" height. The one who appeared the oldest clutched a wooden staff in his hand. Bowing awkwardly and self-consciously, I handed him a sack of gifts that the guide had bought earlier that morning in Kribi and that we had lugged through the forest. The price of our visit.

The headman pulled things out of the bag one by one and dropped them onto the ground. Boxes of matches and bars of soap for the women. Packages of cigarettes and bottles of fermented palm-wine for the men. As the items were shown around, I wished I had bothered to check the gift list with the guide before we left. Here we were, contributing to the delinquency of the Other. When the headman had finished his inspection of the fruits of the western world, he reached out to shake hands with me. As we shook, he took another swig from his bottle of American whisky and passed it along the line. Late morning, and the Pygmy men were already wasted.

By that time, the girls had already intimated to me with facial tics and small gestures that we were not the only visitors that sultry morning. On the other side of the Pygmy village center, huddled close to the women and under the slim shade of a sickly tree, were two *other* whites, an elderly gentleman and a younger woman, both dressed in Alpine hiking gear and bearing knapsacks covered with flaps and buckles. Suffering from a sudden onset of cross-cultural cluelessness, I didn't know how to respond to these two. I felt like Perry when he heard that Amundsen had beaten him to the South Pole, and I didn't even know that we had had competition. Maybe the two were ghosts. Maybe they resented our coming to *their* village, since I knew westerners to be rather proprietary. One thing I knew for sure: they were the source of the Jack Daniels.

We decided to nod in the direction of the other colonials and continue our visit as if *we* were the special guests. The girls and I walked around the tiny village—maybe a dozen little structures surrounded by a half-acre of forest slashed into temporary fields—for about a half an hour. The sun was high and hot, and the women went on about their work. One picked nits or fleas from a child's head, another fanned the smoldering sticks under a blackened cooking pot. Meanwhile, the men drank and giggled. Plastic bottles and sacks and bits of tin and foil crunched underfoot as we walked; the village was awash in trash. Johanna put her digital camera on video mode, and she recorded a guided tour through an empty hut. Most striking to her was the raised bed, about a foot off the ground and no more than five feet in length, made of rows of sticks. As she finished her illustrated narration, she made the mistake of leaning against a support post and almost knocked the fragile structure down. It was time for us to be going.

Before we left, Richard wanted a picture of himself with the village chief, to which I had no objection. Fortunately, he had arranged for that photo op—with no exchange of money or alcohol—and stood smiling broadly next to the fuzzy old man, who leaned on his staff to steady himself. Richard and the Pygmy, Cameroonian man and Baka man. Johanna got the picture.

We decided to shake hands as we departed though I was never sure if the Pygmies shook hands among themselves or found it a curious pastime of visiting ghosts. In the meantime, the *other* visitors had gotten up to inspect the hut that Johanna had almost flattened. I was relieved that we would be able to skip their farewell. Then, lining up one after another, we bent down to touch the palms, one by one, of the women and the men of the village. Up and down the sidelines of the tiny village center we went, our intrepid band of unintentional explorers. No one made eye contact with me; I looked down to the ground as we reached the last group of hands.

The guide led us back without hoots or hoopla on the forest path to our canoe. I stubbed my toe on a root, but otherwise the return was without incident. Once in the pirogue, everyone sat quietly. Whether exhausted from the visit or withered from the heat, I did not know. Gliding easily down the Lobé, we reviewed the landmarks—the shrimp baskets, the monkey trap, the islands, the rocks—that we had met heading up the river. We could hear the falls of the Lobé long before we approached them, and at the last moment the boatman turned into our dark estuary whose guardian trees seemed to part to allow us passage.

The Lobé is but a smaller sibling of the Congo River that Conrad found so eerily compelling and repulsive at the same time. Having travelled a little up our river, I could never find the Lobé and its surrounding forests and their inhabitants to be the antithesis of civilization, as Conrad might have. The real challenges to civilized behavior can much more readily be seen in cities—European or African—rather than in the bush. The mid-sized American city that I call home—like so many post-industrial American urban centers—has fallen on hard times, its businesses boarded up, population poor, schools in trouble. In Cameroon, my family and I live in the capital city Yaoundé, a noisy, cranky place where people show little concern for one another and everyone seems interested only in what he can bilk from his neighbor.

In his tale, Conrad makes mention of "forgotten and brutal instincts" that, he determines, thrive on a diet weak in positive human interaction and rich in natural-animal behaviors. He might make similar remarks while driving through Yaoundé today as taxis whiz by irrespective of any driving courtesy or regulation or while walking through a number of decayed neighborhoods in Evansville, Indiana, my overseas home. The urban wilderness contains no menacing trees or inscrutable bodies of water: its heart of darkness can be heard beating in all those who do not consider the welfare of the people and place of human community, wherever that community struggles to flourish.

Interestingly enough, the Pygmies appear to have missed much of the social upheaval that has come about as a result of the interaction of Europeans and Africans of these parts. And, ironically, they may have become symbols of the "untamable past" or at least of what superior (and, as Conrad suggests, morally inferior) forces could not possess as they extracted so much from these forests and this land. A number of my colleagues would choose to see the Pygmies— and other such groups untouched by "civilizing forces"—as unspoiled and therefore pure. But to see the Pygmy men swaying together in the early morning heat as they swigged whiskey and sucked on cigarettes, I could not see them as spokesmen for the virtues of a healthy, viable civilization. Nor could I consider the relative squalor of their village as example of any social or spiritual superiority. How ironically sad that, in this case, our "gift" of western civilization was a package of its most nugatory vices, wrapped up with money and the promise of more.

But I would go up the Lobé again, and I would visit the Pygmies again, next time with a slightly different shopping list. How important it is that others of us travel up these rivers with their shouldering forests and meet their human inhabitants. How important it is that we try to slough off the prejudices of cultural formation and educational training as we attempt to make our way into the clearing of encounter. For the human imagination can be a dangerous thing, and the greatest thinkers can make fabulous forests into pernicious bogeymen, see poison snakes in waters that produce great life, attribute malicious intentions to inert but fecund wilderness.

NOTES

1. Hochschild, Adam. *King Leopold's Ghost.* Boston: Houghton-Mifflin, 1998.

2. Conrad, Joseph. *Heart of Darkness.* In *A Conrad Argosy.* NY: Doubleday, Doran & Company, 1942. p. 48.

3. Ibid.

Chapter Eleven

Curriculum vitae

While my family and I lived in Yaoundé from 2004 to 2005 we hired a young Cameroonian man to serve as our driver through the tangled welter of roads, occasionally paved and often not, that make up the impossible map of this growing city. Richard Chilla, originally from the northwest province of the country, had been recommended to us by another Fulbrighter, and we learned quickly to value his knowledge of roads and city districts (*quartiers*) in a town where there are no street signs. We began to depend on Richard for much more than basic transportation as well. In many ways Richard became our guide to life in Cameroon.

Richard is hard-working, inquisitive, tactful, and kind. Though from the cooler anglophone part of the country, he has made Yaoundé his home, and he knows the city very well, no small feat. Years ago, Richard was training to become an electrician in a public secondary school program, but he had to withdraw for lack of money. Like many young Cameroonians, he took to driving a taxi. But his years behind the wheel of his little yellow cab only added to his diverse and remarkable list of skills—the cultural education of his world. The brief résumé that I have drawn up for Richard is accurate though not at all complete.

NAME:

Richard Wirdzikire Chilla

PERSONAL:

Born 17 December 1979 in Kumbo, Cameroon

ADDRESS:

No street name or number for the single room with a bare light bulb in the quartier of Yaoundé called Tam-tam Weekend

EDUCATION:

Lower 6th Form, Government Technical High School, Bamenda. Left school in sixth year of secondary study for inability to pay school fees (roughly 30 dollars a year).

LANGUAGES:

Lamnso (fluent—and reading), English (fluent—and reading), Pidgin (fluent), French (speaking ability), Creole (speaking ability), Ewondo (speaking ability)

SKILLS:

- How to tap raffia palms for wine, where to cut the tree, how deep to make the cut, how to collect the liquid
- How to collect the large beetles that come to sip from the wound in the palm trunk and knowledge of where to sell those beetles for food
- How to make an animal trap from a piece of found wire and bamboo, how to catch, skin, and prepare bush rats, porcupines, bush dogs
- How to locate a bed of good clay and make dry-season bricks by wetting the clay, mashing-tamping it, and pressing it into wooden molds then drying them for two days before unmolding
- How to collect and split firewood with a machete; knowledge of which trees produce burnable wood, which trees can be rived, which are better left standing
- How to find water in the dry season (from December through February) by locating thriving raffia palms in low-lying areas, digging nearby, and waiting for water to bubble up to the surface
- How to cull and work bamboo—which types of bamboo are best used whole (for making doors or support poles) and those suitable for making into splint, peeled from dry-standing bamboo and left in water until ready to bend and use
- How to weave splint baskets; how to weave bamboo ceilings, either herringbone or chevron pattern
- How to clear bush with a machete, removing even small trees with repeated cuts and prying out the roots
- How to plant dry-land rice and *njama-njama* (tropical huckleberry), grown in raised beds and flooded each day by opening earthen sluices
- How to cut ripe sugar cane with a machete—carefully avoiding the sharp spikes of the sliced cane—carry it to market, pare the tough outer layers off, to consume or sell
- How to slaughter and skin goats, pigs, sheep by slitting the throat, burning off the bristles, then slicing up the carcass
- How to clean and cook njama-njama with calcium carbonate to soften the taste and texture of the bitterleaf plant
- How to locate, pick, and prepare cola nut and a host of unusual local fruits and nuts

- How to create a slingshot out of bits of blown automobile tires and collect and clean birds for dinner
- How to carry baskets or large sacks (of corn, manioc, cocoyam) on the head, balancing the load while walking up and down bush paths
- How to build a basic brick house by laying bricks, leveling the corners, framing the door and windows with wood, and mudding with wet clay
- How to thatch a hut by creating a flat frame of solid bamboo with slats running horizontally, then stuffing bunches of spear grass just under the bamboo slats until the entire roof is covered
- How to make a beehive out of bamboo and procure the honey by smoking out the bees
- How to drive a stick-shift automobile, even in the crowded traffic conditions of Yaoundé
- Ability to hear pedestrians' requests (yelled out as the passengers wait in large groups at street corners) for taxi rides to specific locations while driving in very heavy traffic
- Knowledge of the location of innumerable quartiers in Yaoundé where no street names are posted and where many of the names are only local, not official
- Knowledge of all named buildings, embassies, and shops in Yaoundé, also nurseries
- Ability to bargain for lowest price for just about anything
- Knowledge of where products are sold in the many outdoor markets of Yaoundé
- Ability to understand and work with Americans

REFERENCES:

Bill Hemminger, Fulbright Professor of Literature, University of Yaoundé I, Yaoundé, Cameroon

Chapter Twelve
O, Christmas Tree

It doesn't take much of a poet to see the temperate wonder of a tree that retains its growing green despite the drop in temperatures and the drop of others' leaves. Something about resistance and resilience in the face of adverse conditions. Something about appearances too, keeping up a green face while everyone else has gone gray-brown, even though the rough weather stresses the evergreen too.

It does take a little poetic imagination, though, to see Christmas in Yaoundé Cameroon Africa, where the onset of the dry season coincides with the first twitches of holiday nostalgia. In its seasonal ebb south from the Sahara, the harmattan wind brings long dry sunny afternoons, uncomfortable though neither oppressively humid nor terribly hot. Not long after that wind has dispelled the heavy rain clouds of the rainy season, the damp red soil that has gulped so much water in September October November turns to pink powder and those puffs of wind that in the rainy season sent cool chills down your back now bring tears to your eyes and a recurrent rasp to your throat. Curiously, the broadleaf trees of the city retain their green into the season. Despite the drought, a few even begin to flower—and dramatically so, like the plumeria. Overhead, green mangoes begin to plump on the shapely mango trees, fruitful decorations for later picking.

The urge to bring a green tree into our home has followed us across the ocean to an unlikely site for Christmas.

Back in our home in the United States, I admit that I have become a Christmas curmudgeon, horrified at the hyper-commercial holiday sell that begins shortly after the witches depart on All Saints' Day and culminates, I suppose, in the orgy of gift returns that takes place the day after what should be for all of us a holy, reflective time. One dignified bit of seasonal preparation does remain, however—the search for a Christmas tree. Each year that we have lived in southern Indiana, my family and I have joined with friends to hunt for the green emblems that will carry us hopeful into the new year.

The first or second Saturday in December, we gather in a city parking lot, swap riders and vehicles, saws and trimmers, gloves and clippers, then restart the convoy and glide into rural Warrick County in search of Christmas trees and greenery, a truly druid activity. For years we have gone to the same spot, lumpy land reclaimed from strip mines whose cousins still actively give up their coal from seams not far below the root reach of these trees. Our friend Alan checks each year with the coal company officials to make sure that we can freely take trees from their land. To be sure, no one else would think of coming this way: the land has been blasted into unnatural, crimped hillocks and sloughs; here and there, slag-heaps still peek out from beneath thin sheaths of grass or sad stands of slash pines; streams run orange and oily with effluent from underground chambers. But, somehow, in the unflattering light of early winter weather, this spot is transformed into the resurrected bit of wildness that provides for each of us a physical reminder of what we see but cannot understand—the miracle of growth under inhospitable circumstances.

And, in southern Indiana, which resides on the frontier between the subtropical South and the reliably-wintry North, that weather can be unpredictable. One year the ice was so thick in the city parking lot that we slipped and fell just divvying up riders and equipment; that year, the wind blew dry-cold in Warrick County, and the late morning sun peered weakly orange from behind streaky purple clouds. Another year, the temperature was so high that we sweated uncomfortably in the long sleeves that we know we should wear for protection against blackberry brambles and clinging thistle heads. More typically, though, the day is cool and gray, the bare spots of mine-land mushy. The perfect place for dogs to run, bound through dirty puddles, decorate themselves with burs and tinsel-like strips of grass or reeds. The place to find a tree stuck up against a mound of coal slag or struggling in a thicket of overpowering grape vine, a tree whose branches might imperfectly circle the trunk or whose crown leans to the right or left or whose mid-section has strangely contracted in unsuccessful competition with neighboring plants. The tree that takes the recycled waste of slag and excavated rubble and makes a green and living statement to the world. That tree.

And so it is that each December my homing device directs my thoughts and me to Warrick County and its cache of unmarketable trees. Needless to say, I have had to redirect that urge this year.

It might come as no surprise for you to hear that the Christmas sell has come to Yaoundé Cameroon Africa too. The great gift of globalization: commercial crap travels everywhere and cheaply too. The big food stores—as opposed to the outdoor markets, where Cameroonians find their food—play nonstop Christmas carols on scratchy-tinny loudspeakers as shoppers pore over stacks of plastic madonnas and packages of ornaments made in Bangladesh. Fancier restaurants—which no ordinary Cameroonian could afford—bear signs urging customers to make their reservations for expensive holiday feasts. And there will be Christmas trees for sale, people have said, evergreens brought in from Europe. Interestingly, the homely white cedar that grows on those reclaimed mine-lands in southern Indiana also grows here, a narrow column of pale green that calls at least two continents—and a tremendous range of growing zones—home. People say that these trees, too, will be up for sale.

But the girls and I thought that a palm might be more appropriate here. A Christmas palm, brought inside from its outdoor stable.

We conscripted Richard and his yellow taxi and drove to one of the plant-yards that we pass each day as we go to the American School of Yaoundé. The manager of the little plot is a tall thin man whom I know pretty well, having stopped many times to ask him about this or that tree or the depth to plant anthuriums or the optimum growing conditions for orchids. Interestingly, when he learned that we wanted a Christmas tree, he directed us to a white cedar (which is not in fact a cedar) hidden behind a small, adjacent cornfield that he tends. The girls and I looked at one another. No, not a tree that we might find in Indiana for our year in Yaoundé Cameroon Africa.

Almost instinctively, the girls and I headed towards a stand of fishtail palms, thick tallish palms with stubby, fin-like fans and strong though flexible dorsal stalks. We walked around and around—as the traffic on the busy road whizzed noisily by—in our appraisal of the tropical goods and selected one that might fill up the space on our balcony that I had reserved for our tree. I asked the price, which was unexpectedly high, and I was happy that Richard entered the bargaining. Soon we reached an agreeable price, and in opening my wallet, I discovered that I had not brought enough money with me. I paid half the price, and we stuffed the palm into the open trunk of the taxi-Toyota. Fronds waved at motorists behind us as we bounced our way back to Bastos, our pricy neighborhood. Richard would return with the rest of the money and a sack for additional soil.

The tree now lives happily in a large container on our balcony, overlooking the building site below and its resident goat. Around the base of the palm, I stuck cuttings from coleus plants, impatiens, and the purple Moses-in-a-basket plant—all of which I snipped from untended alley gardens. So many of our indoor potted plants and outdoor bedding plants grow wild and weed-like in Cameroon. Now, Jill and I greet the Christmas palm tree in the mornings as we drink our coffee on the balcony and watch the day rise over Mont Fébé to the north. The girls and she will decorate the palm a little closer to Christmastime.

We are happy with our holiday tree. I know that the plant man must have been happy with his sale, because he insisted that Richard keep the extra money that I had sent along to pay for the "black soil" planting medium that he creates—sifting plant matter, dirt, and decayed leaves—at the rear of his plant kingdom. As Richard reported, "The plant man gifted me with that money."

And we can contemplate the local gift of green that will live with us into our new year.

Chapter Thirteen
Lost and Found

Our days are typically routine and rather uneventful. Yet, we have just returned from a safari to the distant north of Cameroon, up over the Adamawa Plateau that separates the rainy southern highlands from the arid northern lowlands. And, just a couple of days before we were to leave Yaoundé on the all-night train to the city of Ngaoundéré, gateway to the North, we were robbed at knife-point in the bedroom of our apartment.

THIEF OF NIGHT

Of course, it wasn't supposed to happen to us. In the first place, as the State Department officer who came to help us observed: "Why would anyone want to rob a Fulbrighter, they don't have anything." It is true that we do not live in a villa stuffed with furniture and exotic gewgaws, nor do we even own a car. As further discouragement to would-be thieves: our apartment is up three flights of stairs, and the front balcony faces out onto a courtyard surrounded by high walls, themselves appointed with decorative but imposing metal spears. Then there is the presence of two night guards, one inside the building, the other posted at the big pink gate.

Yet the thief climbed up, slipped through the open sliding glass doors, spent about 30 minutes in our apartment, and—pursued by the State Department officer—jumped off the balcony and scrambled to safety. No guards heard or did anything.

The following recurrent memories may one day become some reconfigured myth, but, in the dark of sleep, they represent signpost moments and elicit powerful feelings these days:

A.) The man wanted to know my name. He kept insisting that I say my name as I came out of my foggy sleep. Then he gave me his—Norton.

B.) Jill had the astonishingly cool presence of mind to slip one of our portable phones into her hand as she begged to go to the bathroom. As I encouraged Norton to move from the dark bedroom to the dark living room, Jill phoned the

US Embassy from the tiled privacy of our little bathroom. Since Fulbrighters are not on the "favored-US citizens" list, the marines who answered the phone were not able to locate our apartment. Resourceful under stress, Jill gave the name of the officer in charge of Fulbright grantees—he lives not far from our apartment—whom the marines then contacted. A peremptory flush and, moments later, Jill was at my side in the living room.

C.) While still in the bedroom (which, naturally, held all the money that we needed for our up-coming trip), Norton began fumbling with one hand—always in the dark—through our things. He got hold of Jill's silver flute and asked her if she were a doctor. *Non, elle n'est pas médecin,* I said. He carefully replaced the flute parts in their case and closed the case.

D.) Despite the fact that Norton initially announced that he was working with gang members who had tied up the guards (a typical tactic; often the guards are complicit with the robbers), I began to doubt his assertion (after about 15 minutes) and, while we were standing in the living room, I slipped open the deadbolt on the apartment door.

E.) Johanna sleeps with the door to her bedroom open; hers is the first bedroom beyond the living room. Norton undoubtedly had stood peering through her doorway before figuring that the parents would be down the hall. Who knows what other thoughts crossed his mind. By the time Jill was out of the bathroom, Johanna had awakened and was crying in her bed. Hearing her crying, Norton told me that he, too, had a daughter. Happily for Mollie, she managed to sleep through the entire episode.

F.) Forgoing Jill's medicine bag and a closet drawer that held an envelope stuffed with stacks of bills that picture simpering Cameroonian men, Norton contented himself with rifling our wallets—collecting about $80—and relieving us of our two cell phones. He insisted that we had a third phone (how could he have known?), which, ironically, would have been true a few days earlier except that one of his countrymen had lifted that phone from our driver's hands as Richard was making a call. So, we had but two phones to offer to our unwanted visitor.

G.) Norton backed us into Johanna's room as he was making ready his escape. Outside, in the central hallway, I could hear a voice calling out our names: it was Walsh, from the State Department. I pushed Jill and Johanna back and came out of the room. Suddenly, the door to the apartment burst open, Walsh yelled out, shone a flashlight into the room, Norton bolted, Walsh sprayed tear gas, Norton threw the knife at Walsh as he hopped over the balcony and got away. The knife and the tear gas canister remained behind as mementos of the visit. I have since thrown away the canister, but the knife—a 12-inch cheap butcher knife whose irregular blade shows all the hallmarks of home-sharpening—leans up against a corner in the back balcony. We have brought it out on occasion to show to guests.

Various Embassy security people showed up not long after, and we all stood outside and below trying to imagine how any human could have climbed up and down those walls. Then, back in the apartment somewhere around 4 a.m., we picked up the living room and returned to bed.

We all went to school—Jill and the girls to the American School, me to the university—that day, despite the shock and the fatigue. The following day—as per our plans—we were on the train to the north.

NIGHT SIGHTSEEING

Every night at about six, a 12-car train leaves Yaoundé for Ngaoundéré. If you are lucky, the trip takes about 14 hours with no breakdowns; if you are luckier, you can afford a couchette sleeper car that will afford a little privacy and a place to lie down.

The train left in the thick of a gathering thunderstorm—purple sky, heavy clouds, distant lightning, high humidity. Snaking its way slowly through the city, the train offered little relief from the oppressive but exciting weather. Everywhere the train passed, people—of all ages—lined up and waved or made silly faces or danced in place. Since the train follows the Mfoundi River out of the city, its rail bed is low and often swampy. Great rivers of trash washed through the valley just outside our elevated windows, and, perched above our heads, rows of shacks clutched nervously to the low hillsides. From behind those shacks little muddy footpaths ran down the hills to a bigger network of paths, some already inundated by the growing rains. Behind other shacks grew huge mountains of trash wrapped up in black plastic sacks and bobbling water bottles. Mollie and I stood transfixed in the train window despite the driving rain.

After several slow kilometers of cityscapes, the train began to pull away from the congested population center. Johanna took her position on an upper bunk, her face inches from the open couchette window, taking picture after picture. Jill sat curled up on a lower bunk, book or crossword puzzle in hand. At the corridor window Mollie and I had to duck inside to avoid being smacked in the face by flashing banana leaves or bright-blooming helianthus plants, a beautifully successful sunny weed in this place. On occasion, the green gave way to reveal homes and huts pressed tightly up against the red earth hill walls. An hour or so into the trip, the storm subsided, and the western rays of the sleep-deprived sun colored the skies above hilly villages and solitary tall, thick-trunk kapok trees.

From that point until we reached Ngaoundéré, more than 600 kilometers to the north, we saw few villages and little unnatural light. To be sure, the train made about 10 stops throughout the night, and in each case you could see the concrete quays come to life before the train reached the stations, which stretch across the lonely map of wet highlands in central Cameroon. The whistle would blow, and in the dark you could make out human figures—back-erect under the weight of a large bowl or basket—scurrying up and down the quays. Food for sale—bananas, pineapples, avocados, mashed manioc wrapped up in banana leaves and sold as *bâtons*, dark local honey collected in plastic liter bottles—and delivered into the myriad hands reaching out from the train windows. "Ana-nana-nana-na," was one woman's musical sales pitch for the ripe pineapples that

she balanced on her head as she ran down the quay. A chorus of variations on
the French word for honey, *miel*: "Mi-yell-e, mi-yell-e." And a chant from little
kids asking for empty plastic bottles—*bouteilles vides*—sung in 6/8 rhythm: *bu-
tay-ye vee-de, bu-tay-ye vee-de*. At some unexpected moment, the train would
lurch forward, people would jump on or back off the train, and the snake would
disappear into its hole in the dark.

And dark it was, not exactly prime conditions for sightseeing. Yet I felt that
I saw a great deal, as if this vast expanse of wooded and open land reveals more
of its empty mystery at night. The loggers have come through, and in their wake
stretch hectares and hectares of scraggly second-or-third-growth trees, more like
the stunted savanna scapes that I expected to see later in the trip. But, much forest still remains, and a dark green curtain surrounded the largest of open fields.
From the distant darkness of my train window I could still see that these tropical
forests so readily arrange themselves in layers. The tallest trees extend enormous
boles 80 or more feet straight up before breaking into aerial arteries of branches,
while more compact trees covered in balls of leaves reach up to their woody
waists, and at the crowded ground below thick tufts of raffia or bamboo snatch
what sun they can from the massive vegetable canopy over their heads. Every
now and then I could make out a little path—once I made out a single night bi-
cycle rider—and the trees would give way to a little clearing and a hut or two
asleep in the dark. Occasionally, the absence of intense dark on the horizon indi-
cated the proximity of the Sanaga River, the largest in Cameroon; train tracks
were planted parallel to the fairly flat river bed for many kilometers. Tarnished
silver, the broad river would come into view, flowing at that moment from nowhere to nowhere, then slip away as the train veered off to Congo and the east.
And all the while a night chorus of insects, *chugga-chugga-chugga*, with occasional percussive shrieks of forest birds.

Dawn came a couple of hours before we reached Ngaoundéré, and Mollie
and I resumed our perch at the window. Jill got our couchette together and assembled our luggage. By this time in the morning, the train had climbed up the
Adamawa Plateau—about 1300 meters, around 4000 feet—which has long since
been given over to cattle raising. The trees were few, and the brush between
trampled down. Like necklaces of brown, the hillsides bore the zigzag traces of
cattle trails. In little protected patches of ground grew corn and cocoyam, carefully staked out and fenced in from the marauding bovines. More vulnerable and
more courageous too, striped amaryllis stuck out their trumpets and strapping
leaves in gracious, flowering acknowledgement of the end of the dry season.

Ngaoundéré, the capital of the Adamawa Province, sits atop the ridge that
separates north and south Cameroon. The barrier is more than geographic: the
northern provinces are mostly Moslem, and that religious connection goes back
hundreds of years more than the relatively recent Christianizing of the southern
provinces. Further, the northern provinces are low, relatively flat, and dry—drier
still as national lands reach up to the Sahara Desert. Interestingly enough, this
part of the country—despite what you might feel would be an inhospitable climate—is, in many places, densely populated. People here have long ago learned

to live—mostly modestly—with the demands of this climate, and they have done well.

Our driver, a Fulfulde-speaking Fulani man from the Extreme North Province, was congenial and knowledgeable. Having lived in the similar Sahelian region of northern Senegal for several years, I felt that I shared a good deal with Aminou. So, as we jounced out of pleasant Ngaoundéré and down the plateau to Bénoué National Park to the north, we talked about Lake Chad, the harmattan wind, dust storms, the cultivation of millet, mangoes (which do very well in such areas), the Hausa people of Nigeria, and religion. I found that I could use some of the greeting—largely Arabic—that worked in villages in northern Senegal as I talked with Aminou and others, a pleasant cultural and linguistic surprise.

The first peek over the plateau revealed a low-lying land that literally steamed in the late-morning sun. The moment we picked for visiting the park was best for viewing wildlife but also the hottest, most humid time of year—those yearning months when moisture from the Gulf of Guinea, already pounding the southern cities with rain, runs out of steam at the Adamawa Plateau, expending itself on the plains below in days of increased humidity with no possibility of precipitation. Daily highs reach 105 degrees easily, and the nights simmer down to a rather uncomfortable 85 degrees. Amazingly, in anticipation of the rains (which may come in mid-April though more usually in May), many trees had put on a cloak of light green leaves, though the ground was bone-dry and hard. Amazingly also, the mango trees were producing fruit: the densely thick trees that adorned just about every hut gave up buckets of fruits that we found in little piles along the road. Mollie and I ate great quantities of them. Jill and Johanna had hoped to see baobab trees, but the great markers of almost-desert regions prefer drier conditions, where they have little arboreal competition. The few baobabs we saw stood thin and undistinguished.

About two hours north of Ngaoundéré we saw the sign for Bénoué National Park. We stayed on the main road (there is only one paved road in northern Cameroon) for a good 50 miles or so until we reached the turn-off to the park. The road quickly deteriorated into a rocky dirt track, and we drove for 24 miles before reaching the official entrance to the park. This is one big park. At the entrance is the Buffle Noir, what the French call a *campement*—a collection of round huts, a hotel-bar, and several outbuildings. Several baboons came to sit on the porch outside the hotel and inspect us as I made arrangements for our rooms and meals. Jill, the girls, and I then stood outside looking at the dry Bénoué River bed—in the month of March an enormous chasm of folded metamorphic rocks and intervening sandy platforms stretched between two brown wooded banks. The bottom of what would soon be a raging river was now parched dry and hot. Little dots of water below to slake the thirst of tired forest animals or birds.

Aminou told us that the best times for viewing game were dusk and dawn, so we hopped into the 4 x 4 at about 5 p.m. that day for our first sightings of fauna. Bénoué Park is not located in the Sahel—in the rainy season it gets too much rain, about 35 inches—so its landscape is not the characteristic barren stretches of open grass plains punctuated by big thorny trees. Instead, the land is rolling, crisscrossed with rocky stream beds and covered with many trees, none very tall. Since the rainy season had not yet begun, the grass cover was dry and cropped, the stream beds dry. But in a few weeks, the park would become an impenetrable maze of muddy estuaries and tall concealing elephant grass. This was the right moment for our safari.

The animals in Bénoué are not found in large herds. Rather, the disposition of the land and its vegetation favors small groups of animals or individuals. And we saw many animal families. Johanna spent her time leaning out the vehicle window taking photographs—more than 600 during the several days that we were away (thank god—or allah—for digital cameras and the editing function). We learned right away that antelopes, ruminant mammals of the cattle family, come in many forms. Unlike those of our deer at home, the horns of antelopes are not branched, nor are they shed. Among the largest of the antelopes, the bushbucks have great spiral horns several feet in length. A relative of the more familiar wildebeest (AKA gnu), the hartebeest looks more like a horse than an antelope, at least to us other-worlders. Marsh antelopes include the many varieties of kob, deer-like creatures with solid or striped ruddy hides and straight long horns. Smaller antelopes include the Oribi and the Red-flanked Duiker, to which the biologists refer as *Cephalophus*.

Baboons appeared from behind trees and thickets in a number of places as we bounced through the late-afternoon dusty heat. Aminou then took us to a spot on the Bénoué River where enough water had collected to make a perennial pool, liquid home to a host of hippopotami. Rapacious flies strafed us on the high rocks as we looked down into the muddy hole and shouted ridiculous human words of greeting at the still waters. At first, only a few distended snouts stuck out. Then, those grand toothy heads revealed themselves to us; one female stepped up out of the water so that we could see that she was pregnant (Aminou told us so). Sidling up the steep dry river bank at night, these hippos would later leave their day-time bath to follow tortuous paths in search of dry-grass grazing. We knew that we wouldn't want to encounter one of these behemoths on some night journey.

More amazing to me was the avian life. We never saw flocks of birds, generally individuals or couples. But they are some of the most colorful, striking creatures I had ever seen. Early on the afternoon visit, Jill noticed a flash of blue that resolved itself onto a nearby tree branch: it was an Abyssinian Roller, with a sky-blue body outlined with royal blue feathers, a tawny breast, and a scissor-like tail that forks behind the airborne bird. Aminou pointed out a Little Green Bee-eater, a bird of the most mellow chartreuse feathers with highlights of darker green and a slice of black along the inside of the wing. As their name implies, these birds feed on bees and wasps, which they catch in mid-air then smash to death (and to bits) against tree trunks and branches before swallowing the pieces. As we came out of a rocky dip in the road, two Northern Ground-Hornbills lumbered their way through the bush. What extraordinary creatures:

more than two feet tall, with huge protruding bills surmounted by what biologists call a *casque*, the birds looked like an elderly married couple conversing casually on their way to a funeral, all solemn and serious. Aminou stopped the vehicle and ran towards them, trying to urge the stodgy hornbills to flight. Irritated at this disturbance, the pair took off: their enormous white-tipped wings flapped and their red wattles dangled in the hot afternoon air as these magnificent birds took to the air.

We went out again the following morning at sunrise. No problem waking Johanna and Mollie: they were ready for more animals and more sightseeing from inside the 4 x 4. At first, the going was slow. None of us was much awake, and the bush seemed particularly monotonous and empty. More dry grass, more rocky washes, more desolate knolls. We took a turn down a steep hill; the track smoothed, and the hill flattened out. And there they were—a family of giraffes. Tall, sleek, well-suited to the mottled drape of background trees, the beasts almost slipped our attention. But they had seen us. One of the larger giraffes galloped to a distant tree, snipped a branch, then paused. By then, we all had seen—and gasped. The other family members ambled towards him. The car had become silent, a metal shell with breathless animals inside. How gracefully the giraffes moved in this open terrain, those great legs effortless locomotors. Cautiously but intentionally, the group stepped away through the bush. The sentinel male stayed behind, attached to his tree-breakfast, then gamboled after the others when Aminou revved the motor of the vehicle.

Of the other animals we know we saw, here is the list: warthogs (a fast-moving group of three; *phacochère* is their name in French), gazelles, bushbucks, waterbucks, pygmy antelopes. The list of birds is greater: Openbill Stork, Cattle Egret (the colloquial French name, *pic-boeuf,* indicates a primary activity of these birds who hang around kine, feasting on the insect life attracted to the bovines), White-throated Francolins (quail-like ground-hugging birds), Senegal Eremomela (small warblers), Blue-bellied Roller (almost as thrilling as its cousin from Abyssinia), Spotted Creeper (that, like our nuthatch, climbs head-down tree trunks), Blue-breasted Kingfisher (small and ferociously blue), White-browed Robin-chat (like our robin an accomplished singer with a rufous breast), Adamawa Turtle-dove, Grey Kestrel (falcon-like and brown), Black-headed Weaver (whose round reedy nests with small round open doors hang like ornaments on thorny trees everywhere), and the Stone Partridge (a round blackish bird that forages and nests in rocky cliffs around the Bénoué River).

We did not spend the following night at Buffle Noir—Jill and I withered in the night heat—but drove back up to Ngaoundéré, where we found a delightful *auberge* to spend the night. The inn had been built—in a secluded spot—for the use of European hunters who would come to Cameroon, spend days in the hot animated lowlands, then repair to the cool highlands for relaxation and nights of drunken bragging. Those days are gone (happily), the original owner died, and the place fell into desuetude. Having re-opened only two years ago, the Ranch of Ngaoundaba offers charming rooms in a beautiful, quiet, rural setting; the inn and its attendant thatched huts all look down to a crater lake, alive even in the dry season with teeming bird life. Though the air at the Ranch was much cooler and conducive to sleep than in Bénoué Park, I found that I could not sleep well (in fact, neither Jill nor I slept much in the days—and nights—that passed after the robbery). So, somewhere in the middle of the night, I slipped outside our door—under the overhanging canopy of flowering bougainvillea and jasmine vines—and onto the verandah behind the inn. There was somewhat of a moon that night, and everything was bathed in a grayish glow. And the sounds and songs of so many birds—no human voices here to be heard. The Hemmingers spent another wonderful day at the auberge, then found our way back to the all-night train and home in the tropical forests of the south.

GOOD NIGHTS

How wonderful for us to see wildlife in an unfettered habitat; to know that the hornbills could flee from us and resume their stolid march through the un-munchable grass; to watch the giraffes watching us warily but without any obvious human limit to their running; to sense that the antelopes' skittish behavior was a recognition that we humans likewise belong to the class of wild beasts; to sit astonished at the fabulous palette of feather-color and the inventive designs of horns and hoofs; for a moment to glimpse life not regulated by train schedules and morning bells, not measured by unrealistic expectations or shallow successes.

The return train trip took us through night-time landscapes again, only this time the rail safari slogged through great thunderstorms and much rain as it made its way across the un-urban highlands. From time to time, the voices of *miel*-sellers and night birds sang out and will remain with me for a long time.

Though we were relieved to get back to cool Yaoundé, our temporary home, the return to the apartment was not without apprehension. But Jill and I soon realized that we had come a long way since the theft.

I remember that, the night of the robbery and throughout much of the following day, my ears filled regularly with music—the *Lux aeterna* section of John Rutter's *Requiem,* a composition whose gentle, lapping rhythms complement its hopeful text. I guess it should come as no surprise that imagined music might have calmed the night-time of my fears.

Jill's experience was a little different. She was taking a shower in the apartment the day after the break-in and suddenly became painfully cognizant of the fact that she was all alone. But her rising anxiety was quieted by the very palpable presence of Mary Fran, our good friend who had died just before we came to Cameroon. Jill said that she could make out that head of soft white hair and that generous human spirit, and she felt at once at ease and calm.

Nights are better now. They have always offered us occasions to discern what daylight keeps us from seeing.

Chapter Fourteen

Interaction

Our driver Richard pulls up to a busy intersection in Mokolo, one of the very crowded residential districts in Yaoundé. Actually, it is a roundabout, its central hub a pile of defunct truck tires piled up. The traffic whirls, taxis cut in and out. Suddenly we have become part of the surging metal mob that shares the round-about with bold pedestrians, a group of frightened sheep, bicycles, and hand-pulled two-wheel carts loaded with goods. Richard noses through the heavy cur-rent, then breaks away on one of the spoke-roads. Soon he jerks the taxi off to the side of the road, backs into an impossibly narrow space between a perma-nently parked truck and what I call a portable boutique, and stops. We have come to visit the family of the boutique's proprietor.

The man's name is Magellan. He is a relative of Richard's, and he must be close to 40 years of age. He is not tall, and other than his bad teeth, he appears fit and strong. The boutique—actually a make-shift wooden cabinet maybe three-feet square sitting atop an impermanent pedestal of cement blocks and supporting a colorful umbrella for shade from the hot sun—contains Magellan's inventory, proceeds from the sale of which he uses to feed a family. For sale are little packages of biscuits (about 20 cents each), boxes of matches (a few pen-nies), and individual cigarettes (most cost about two cents, the fancier Roth-schilds about five). As we stand there, a man comes up, pays little attention to the three of us talking, removes a cigarette, mutters something to Magellan, then leaves. "He will pay me later," Magellan says. No income with that exchange.

After we have spoken a few words in greeting, Magellan closes and locks up the wooden shelves. He nods to a fellow vendor as if to say, "Please watch this, I will be back." Then we turn down the path to his home. As we walk, Ma-gellan tells me how to make a boutique such as his a success. "You have to come every day at the same time, so people will know you are there. They count on you." The open sewer that parallels our walkway keeps me from paying close attention to his words, however: rainy season water keeps the channels always wet and stinking; occasionally, log-jams of waste make little green lakes alongside someone's concrete-block house. The path descends precipitously: we step over earthen barriers built to divert water, dodge broken sewer-covers. In front of one home, a small triangle of open earth supports a brave papaya tree; the triangle is outlined with a row of small purple-flowering plants: someone here has a yard and keeps it.

Magellan talks, I closely watch the way my feet must go, and people closely watch us passing by. Magellan acknowledges no one as we walk. We pass a young woman—she is seated practically in the path—who speaks in French to two young children, both naked. A fastidious and imperious preacher—wearing clerical collar and black—stomps up the path, Bible in hand. We pass the neighborhood miller—more of a grinder, really—where women line up to crush their pumpkin seed (for *egusi,* a tasty dish of pounded seed and fish), peanuts, and other things piled in their enamel bowls. Buildings—none much taller than a man's or woman's height—crowd alongside the pathway; some face away, some are set slightly above with a stoop extending to the path. At one point I must step over a large aluminum pan filled with manioc roots cooked and left outside to cool, while just behind are piled the remains of the first pressing of palm oil kernels, bright firm red berries that clutch together in thick heads when hanging from the beautiful oil palm, reduced to stringy orange shreds after the oil is squeezed from them. "We are close," Magellan tells me.

There is a small billboard labeled "Plan of the neighborhood" at the corner before the turn to Magellan's house. The carefully-gridded plan bears no resemblance to the maze of foot-paths, drainage canals, and connected shacks that we have just slipped through. Some politician's "master plan" that bears no relation to the lives of real people here. At this point Magellan tells me that he majored in geography—at the university where I teach—before marrying and moving into this slum. I wonder what has happened to someone who has gone so far academically yet lives in such reduced circumstances. I will not ask.

We turn to enter the small muddy space that separates several houses and brings together several families. Kids run to hide in their mom's skirts as they catch sight of me, a rare visitor. Magellan says a few words, the little girls come forward, they shake my hand reluctantly, and we all enter the house.

The place occupies four rooms, all chipped concrete surfaces painted faded dirty blue and red. An entry-way-cum-kitchen, about six feet square, contains a couple of blackened marmites (big cast-iron kitchen pots made for sitting directly on a fire), a few stirring tools, a sieve, and a few baskets. Some clothing hangs from nails pounded into the soft concrete. We walk through to the slightly-larger sitting room, whose ceiling bears the signs of widespread water leaks, and I am shown a bamboo seat. A little window near the ceiling affords the only light; a large wound in the wall behind my chair reveals its constituent wattle sticks that scarcely hold the remaining concrete in place; there is a musty smell, punctuated from time to time when smoke from outside cooking fires wafts in.

By now the girls have gotten used to me, and they make us all laugh as they accept to sit on my knee or answer my questions in English and in French. Adèle is Magellan's youngest—about three years old and bright; Sully her cousin is four, an addition to a family that cannot refuse to house a relative even though they have so little. Magellan tells me that he is proud that Sully lives with him. Eventually, the other children come out to meet me—Carolle, in middle school, and Jerome, 18. Magellan whispers something to Jerome, who disappears for a time, then returns with large bottles of soft drinks, a healthy bunch of bananas, and a bottle of Scotch. Though from an English-speaking part of the country, Ernestine, his wife and Richard's sister, cannot understand my English and looks alternately pained and embarrassed as I try to talk to her. I make an obvious joke; we laugh; the stress is relieved. Though I am warm and not a fan of Scotch, I take a good-sized glass of the special stuff whose vintage is improved through the great generosity of its givers.

Magellan and his family are anglophone, from the Northwest Province. Magellan tells me that they do not get on well with the neighbors, who are distrustful of them, neither French-speaking (though everyone in the family speaks some French) nor from the Center Province. There is such tribal rivalry and inter-ethnic distrust in this country of more than 200 ethnic groups. Yet, Magellan's family manage in this environment. When she is not making cooking fires and preparing meals of *ndolé* (a strong-flavored green that is prepared with meat or fish) or *folong* (another green, milder and similarly prepared), Ernestine makes up little packages of peanuts that she wraps in plastic, spreads on a large colorful platter, then sells along the busy street above. She might make a couple of pennies for every sale she makes. Though he had been doing well in school—the industrial training track in the government high school—Jerome had to withdraw from school last year in order to bring some money home as well. Each day, this strong young man gets up early, then walks in his thin translucent green plastic sandals to local vendors—bars and bigger shops—to get orders for crates of bottles that he then buys elsewhere and lugs in a two-wheel cart back through relentless traffic to the vendors. If the vendor is honest, Jerome will make 50 francs for each crate, about ten cents, and in a good day he will be able to add about a dollar to the family income.

At one point, I take Jerome aside and ask him what he most would like to do. "To go back to school, to finish high school, take the *bac* (the baccalauréat, high-school leaving exam, which is administered in the English system here as well) and get a job as an electrician," he tells me. On the table in the sitting room that serves as dining table, work bench, and study desk, a copy of *Oliver Twist* sits dog-eared and open, Jerome's current reading material. I wonder how Dickens' descriptions of the lively dreadful social underworld of nineteenth-century London seem to a young man whose living conditions may well be worse. Yet, this concrete house is what the working poor of Cameroon afford. I want Jerome to have his chance to go to school.

The Scotch does not fog my mind so much that I forget to thank my hosts for their gifts of hospitality. How is it that people are brought together when we live in such different and, in many ways, opposed worlds? I have decided that my family and I will try to overcome some of that opposition.

At Easter, Mollie and Johanna decorate a few hard-boiled eggs, and with some candy and small gifts that Jill has bought make Easter baskets that we three deliver to those little girls, Adèle and Sully. The three of us—Johanna, Mollie, and I—crammed in that tiny dingy living space, Johanna making funny faces and jokes in English and everybody laughing. Maybe the best gift is two small chalkboards with a pack of colored chalk—so that the girls might practice letters, drawing, counting. At first Adèle and Sully do not know what to make of their chalk boards, but Magellan has since seen to it that the girls know what to do with their gift. The last time I visited the family, the chalkboards bore wobbly numbers; nearby on the table sat pieces of chalk worn down to little nibs.

Some days later I ask Richard to look into the cost of sending Jerome to school. Here is the cost-list:

1) School fees—15,000 francs plus 3,000 F entrance fee
2) C.A.P. registration—13,500 F (the C.A.P. is the exam at year's end)
3) G.C.E. technical—18,000 F (General Certificate of Education, the equivalent to O-level exams in the British system)
4) School uniform—10,000 F (required)
5) Books:
 Electrical Installation Calculation, Vol. III, by A.J. Watkins—5,000 F
 Ordinary Level Mathematics—5,000 F
 Electrical Installation Theory and Practice—5,000 F
 Schéma en électricité—3,000 F
 Five ledgers and five exercise books—12,500 F

Total (for one year): 90,000 F—roughly $180.

Working with Magellan and Richard, we have worked it out so that Jerome can attend the government school in Kumbo, located in the Northwest Province. He has relatives there, he would have a decent place to stay, and since the region is a farming one he would be assured of work (in the family fields) and food.

And maybe the hope of a more comfortable life.

Chapter Fifteen
Visiting God's Village

The villagers call their home Njavnyuy. A few kilometers before you reach the city of Kumbo on a high lava plateau in the Northwest Province of Cameroon, the rugged path to the village splinters off from the main Ring Road that runs in a wide circuit around Mount Oku, at almost 10,000 feet the second highest peak in Cameroon. The Ring Road runs through some of the most beautiful and most populous portions of this nation. More than 360 km in length, the road links mountain communities of peoples speaking a number of languages, many of them Lamnso speakers like the residents of Njavnyuy. Despite linguistic differences, the people share a common occupation—raising a variety of crops and animals on the steep, mostly grassy hillsides. Produce from their farming villages sits for sale in wooden stalls alongside the roadway—firewood, mostly eucalyptus, split into 3-foot post-lengths (suited to outdoor cooking rings); woven baskets and carrying bags made of fur or leather; bananas in massive green bunches still attached at the stem; bunches of tender young carrots, heads of blanched cabbage, cobs of corn suspended from browning husks.

I never imagined that this place might be the caffeine capital of the world as well. Yet, just about every form of popularly-ingestible caffeine grows here or very nearby.

Coffee bushes, sprouting from old tree stock, grow companionably close to every home. The plants are trimmed to a human height, convenient for culling the beans—encased in red cherries—from the slender plants, the first step in the tedious process of removing layer after layer of material from the pale bean inside. Like the Ethiopian highlands, ancestral home of coffee, these African highlands also support the cultivation of the arabica bean, the most particular and most prized of the coffee beans. *Coffea arabica* is quite demanding of its environment in a number of ways. Though able to survive only in tropical regions, it cannot stand great heat or excessive sunlight. Consequently, it is grown as an understory plant, one that grows only in the mitigating shade of overarching leafy trees. Coffee is also a thirsty plant—needing at least 60 inches of rain annually—and its roots demand rich tilth and plentiful oxygen. The villages till the soft, rich volcanic soil into charmingly irregular undulating rows to accommodate the growing demands of their coffee.

At the lower, somewhat sweatier elevations, cacao thrives in the form of smallish trees whose trunks and branches, at the proper time of the year, are strung with cacao pods like Christmas tree ornaments—pudgy red, orange, and yellow-brown dangles about four inches in length. Along paved roads to the village, you pass patches of pods that have been cracked open and spread on the berm to dry in the sun; their perfume is cloyingly sweet as the pods pass through this stage in their metamorphosis into the oily-sweet confection that we know as chocolate. The cacao plant made its way to choice European colonies after Cortez had stolen knowledge of it from the Aztecs in the sixteenth century. In Cameroon, cacao grows readily and, in earlier years, contributed much to the economic importance of the region.

A couple of hours' ride on dusty and breath-taking roads beyond the village, a tea plantation thrives at the 6000-foot elevation of the highlands near the town of Ndu. Riding higher and higher on the rutted road, you think that you cannot possibly take another minute of the bouncing or the powdery red dust that coats your clothes as well as your throat. It is late December, and it has not rained for about two months. But then, just beyond a tall stand of columnar airy eucalyptus, the pavement picks up again and, spread alongside the tarmac, fields of tea clothe the hillsides in peaceful green. The tea plant, *Camellia sinensis*, bears shiny evergreen leaves like those of its ornamental relative, the flowering camellia, whose fragrant exotic winter-flowering shrubs can be found almost as far north as Indiana. But the fabulous flowers will not appear here. *Camellia sinensis*, when kept cropped on waist-high shrubs, bears little leaves that—when picked, aged, and decocted—become the familiar English Breakfast, Lipton, and other beverages that find their way to tables everywhere in the world. Like a vast knee-high lawn, the plants cover hillside after hillside; the fields are stitched together with strips of eucalyptus and cedar that, similarly, carry their green wraps into the dry season. And, out across the ocean of diminutive but ancient plants, waves of workers pick their way through the fields, selecting only the smallest leaves at the very growing edge of the stems then deftly depositing the caffeinated crop into loosely-woven baskets.

Less well-known to visitors is the cola nut, which figures prominently in social history in this part of Africa. The cola tree, related to the cacao, grows tall and thick here, its giant boles covered in patchy lichens that attest to the high rainfall and year-round humidity in the village. High up in the tree, large soft-ball-sized sacks shield a cargo of reddish "nuts" that, like garlic, break up into little hard nuggets when brought down and dried. Sucked and masticated, these nuggets are regularly given as gifts—to visitors, to those about to depart on a voyage, to newly-weds. The nuts have given their name to the original recipe of Coca Cola, whose astringent caffeine jolt (partly masked by the addition of sugar or its chemical substitute) has been addicting Americans for many years. Similarly, the cola nut has been chewed—despite its chalky flavor and puckering potential—for the caffeine it contains as well as its shot of glucose. There are many stories of local people whose hunger or thirst was slaked as they sucked on a cola nut: the nut works as both stimulant and appetite suppressant. In this naturally opulent world, it is hard to imagine that people here could be hungry, so fecund is the vegetable growth that seems to thrive irrespective of human intervention. Perhaps, in this way, the cola nut reminds villagers of their dependence on the green world and its sustaining gifts.

We arrived in Njavnyuy a couple of days after Christmas. Jill and the girls wanted to celebrate Christmas at home in Yaoundé, and though typically restless in cities, I did not object. So, we left Yaoundé very early on the morning of the 26th, stopping in the city of Bafoussam to visit Richard's brother and his wife and to enjoy a big meal of njama-njama (local greens cooked with pork or beef in palm oil), chicken in a wonderful red sauce (tomatoes, palm oil, and local herbs), and maize fufu (something like hand-held polenta). We spent a night in the capital of the Northwest Province, Bamenda, and had several fine hours with Richard's sister, Hilda, who runs a little restaurant-bar called Festival. The following day we began our trek along the Ring Road, mostly paved, often rutted and dusty, always beautiful.

Our yellow taxi, Richard's vehicle, bounced into Njavnyuy around two o'clock in the afternoon. Though the village sits a kilometer or so off the main road, word of our arrival reached the village long before we finally lurched down the road—scarcely more than an enlarged dirt path—and flopped to a stop in front of Richard's family compound. I cannot say what was more striking— the crowd of adults and children that surrounded us as we unfolded ourselves from the compressed conditions of the taxi or the surrounding palisade of stout ochre walls of the compound buildings. The vertical walls stretch directly up to a horizon of corrugated roof panels (people here call them *zinc*) that pour down water onto the bright red hardpan of the compound yard during the rainy season. The orange-red of the yard and its attendant buildings sets off the bright green of the neighboring coffee plants; within a few yards in any direction you can see oranges ripening in their round shapely trees, a copse of cola trees, bunches of banana trees whose leaves shiver in the slightest breeze, and little rectangular patches of cultivated greens.

We were overtaken by the family, though. Hands reached through open car windows as we approached the compound; once we disembarked, we stood still as the hands came at us one after the other. That these people were laborers you could tell by their hands—the damp bony hand of the woman who had just left the blackened cooking pot on the fire; the thick cozy hand of Richard's father, a healthy and genteel 74 years of age; the dirty paws of kids who had just come from lugging water or chopping kindling; and the rough muscular mitt of the palm wine tapper, a neighbor and good friend of the family. One neighbor woman, in particular, could not stop thanking us for coming—as if their hospitality was in some way a gift from us—and repeatedly grabbed my hand, shaking it vigorously in her own each time.

And such warm smiles. It had been several years since Richard had been to his village, and you could tell by the look of surprise and pleasure that his welcome was very special. En route to Njavnyuy, Richard pulled the taxi up to a little house alongside the road; inside the compound, a young woman was bent over, sweeping the red yard with the bound whorl of thin sticks that serves as a broom here. He honked the horn, she glanced up, saw only a taxi full of strangers, returned to her work. He honked again, she stopped her work and approached the vehicle, puzzled. The moment that she descried Richard, she screamed, threw down the broom, broke into a run, grabbed him and hugged him through the little Toyota window, then ran around the taxi, shaking our hands one by one and chattering excitedly in Lamnso. We were all welcome.

Of the many experiences that we had in Njavnyuy in the space of only several days I will describe only one—tapping palm wine.

We woke up too late in the morning to accompany the tapper on his regular rounds, so he made a point of coming round to get us later in the morning. The nights at this elevation are uncomfortably cool, even by my polar standards, and I had spent much of the night shivering even though we were given beds, blankets, and a room with a door that closed tightly. And then the matins splash of water, dredged up from its 54-degree vein in the earth. It was chilly. But we were all ready to go when the tapper called.

In this area, palm wine is made from the raffia palms. Unlike the oil palms, whose tappers—as Chinua Achebe has famously described—must climb high up the palm to make their incisions, the raffia palm is tapped at the point where the fleshy fronds separate from the ground. The raffia palm—whose fronds, when dried, provide the papery strips that folks at home might recognize—looks like a palm without a trunk: tall, feathery leaves grow right out of the soil in great clumps that reach 15 or 20 feet.

On our way to the raffia palms we passed through a large checkerboard of small, irrigated fields. On this relatively flat plain, in the two or three months of dry weather, the village women channel mountain water around a network of raised garden beds. What interested me was not only what the women had planted in the beds—huckleberry (a source of greens and, in this country, a member of the tomato family, *Solanum*), sweet potatoes, and cabbage—but also all the edible plants that come up on their own. In this last group are *Colocasia esculenta* (ornamental elephant ears now popular in flower gardens at home) whose characteristic ears pop up anywhere the soil is cleared, tomatoes (from last year's garden perhaps), and watermelons. And, I learned later, these fields represent only a portion of the family's cultivated land; the more significant acreage covers a distant mountainside. In fact, the day we left the village, most of the remaining family members were heading out—on foot—to the fields where they would stay for several weeks as they worked and harvested the dry-season crops.

We stepped gingerly through the fields, said hello to the women, and made our way to the raffia palms where the tapper was already at work. With his machete, he makes a deep cut on a choice fleshy stem just above the ground level.

Suddenly, a milky sap gathers and drips freely from the wound; the tapper jams the glass or plastic jug he has brought for this purpose between the earth and the tree (he knows the precise height and angle to make the cut so that no juice is lost); and in a matter of minutes he has a quart or two of sugary sap. The sap is nutritious and begins to ferment almost instantly. Within a couple of hours, the alcohol content is about 4%; in a couple of days, the sweet stuff has become vinegar. In the several days of our visit to Njavnyuy, we had palm wine at just about all stages of its potable life. When fresh, it is pleasant; a day later, it is almost dangerous.

Palm wine—and its collecting—are important parts of social life in the village. Richard's father Nicolas belongs to a Secret Drinking Society, whose drinking is really not much secret at all, especially since the society men often gather in the home of Nicolas' deceased father just behind the current family compound. His father's house sits squarely in the center of several fields; two paths cross just in front. Nicolas explained that three of his father's four wives are buried at this crossroads (or, more accurately, crosspaths), one wife at each corner. These three corners now support a thick growth of crops, while the fourth corner—the future home of the wife who is still much alive, usually hunched inside the cooking house next to the smoky warm fire—bears a couple of stumps that are used as resting spots by passersby. It would be difficult, in village tradition, to wander far from the influence of family members, living or not.

But, the living is not all easy in the village. The simple wooden doors of the compound buildings—if they house children—are marked in white chalk with a hieroglyphic assortment of numbers, slash-marks, and letters. These are the telltale signs of polio brigades that have recently come through these remote villages since several outbreaks of polio have been recorded in nearby Nigeria. The health workers came to inoculate children against the disease that many had hoped had been eradicated. Yet this is only one of a number of diseases—malaria, rheumatic fever, dysentery—that claim the lives of so many of these children.

And then the children themselves—so many children. A line from a famous Robert Frost poem defines *home* as the place you know that you can go when there is nowhere else to turn. Nowhere is this observation truer than in Njavnyuy. Several adult daughters of Nicolas and his wife Hildegard have returned to the village after years of living elsewhere—probably in crowded cities like Bamenda or Yaoundé. One daughter, a tall attractive woman, has returned to Njavnyuy with three children—who have, as Richard says, various fathers and no father—who will be brought up on the very limited budget of the village compound. The same is true of several other sisters, and as a result there is a welter of young people who fill the compound with noise and play. But there is little financial support for these kids, who may be loved and fairly well fed, but who must also be clothed and sent to school or church.

And yet the children figure in my fondest memory of Njavnyuy. In the village, night falls quickly—just after six—and, as usual, the generator in town was

on the blink when we were visiting. The result: a thorough darkness unlike anything most of us will ever experience in the perma-glow of our electrified
worlds. Despite the throngs of stars, the sky looked back black at us, and the
ruddy ground absorbed what little radiant energy emanated from so far away.
Richard's younger brother brought out the hurricane lamps, located some kerosene, set the wicks, and the yellow globes shown warmly though dimly for us
all. We set the lamps here and there around the compound, each one illuminating a small circular world of its own. The older women stayed in the cooking
hut, washing out pots and preparing for the next day's meal. Meanwhile, the
children decided to sing.

One of the older girls—who had obviously sung in a church choir—led the
kids in several hymns. The youngest children—Vera and a little boy, both tod-
dlers—were strapped to the backs of their just-older siblings, a strip of cloth
used as a cinch. A couple of older boys—Pius and Prince William—stood off to
the side and behind, but they too took part in the singing. The tempo quickened,
and Miranda, the leader, decided to start to dance. A dancing song—the kids
form a circle, clap and sing, while the one whose name has been sung must enter
the circle and dance her dance. More singing, much clapping. The lights flick-
ered, and childish shadows became suddenly profound. It was as if the world
centered on this place, at this time, where the children of this world were singing
out their parts. One by one, the kids' names were called, and each one danced,
even Pius. Nicolas sat off to the side, leaning against the building he had probably built, whose constituent bricks he had undoubtedly formed from the clay of
this compound. The light shone on his big frame and his kind face. The older
women talked quietly in the cooking shed. The rest of us let the children in us
dance in the private dark of that evening.

We got up early the next day to leave Njavnyuy, despite repeated requests
that we stay. We shook hands around, and Richard's mother grabbed Jill and
gave her a big hug. Nicolas gave us a hand-made basket to take back with us,
and one of Richard's brothers put a sack of new potatoes and cola nuts into the
back of the taxi. It was a quiet ride back to Bamenda, but somewhere in the road
dust I asked Richard if, in Lamnso, the name of his village had any particular
significance. "Njavnyuy means, 'God shares,'" he said. After what we had seen,
tasted, and touched in the village, I felt I understood.

INDEX

www.ingramcontent.com/pod-product-compliance
Lightning Source LLC
Chambersburg PA
CBHW021822270326
41932CB00007B/303